food from fire

food from fire

the real barbecue book

Charles Campion

photographs by Jason Lowe

MITCHELL BEAZLEY

Food from Fire

by Charles Campion

First published in Great Britain in 2006
by Mitchell Beazley, an imprint of
Octopus Publishing Group Limited,
2–4 Heron Quays, London E14 4JP

A CIP catalogue record for this book is
available from the British Library.

ISBN 13: 978 184533 203 7

ISBN 10: 1 84533 203 2

While all reasonable care has been taken
during the preparation of this edition, neither
the publisher, editors, nor the authors can
accept responsibility for any consequences
arising from the use thereof or from the
information contained therein.

Commissioning Editor:
Rebecca Spry

Executive Art Editors:
Nicky Collings, Yasia Williams-Leedham

Design:
Miranda Harvey

Editor:
Vanessa Kendell

Photography:
Jason Lowe

Home economy:
Trish Hilferty

Production:
Angela Young

Index:
John Noble

Printed and bound by
Toppan Printing Company in China

Thank you

It's all very well basking in the joys of finishing a book,
but despite whoever is listed as 'author' on the title page,
all good books are a collaborative effort. Bringing out a
book takes a surprisingly long time, and this one is no
exception. Between the first glint of an idea and its arrival
on the bookshop shelves, a great many different people
have worked exceedingly hard. So the most important job
an author ever faces is writing the thank-yous!

Effusive thanks are due to Rebecca Spry and Yasia
Williams-Leedham of Mitchell Beazley. Miranda Harvey not
only designed a stunning book but also made good bread.
Vanessa Kendell handled the painstaking job of copy editor.
Photographer Jason Lowe ignored the inclement weather
and took beautiful pictures, while Trish Hilferty cooked
delicious food for those photos. Jason Lowe and Lori de
Mori allowed their peace to be invaded for the duration of
the shoot, as did Mr. Bruni and Felicity Carter of Val de
Chalvane. Thomas, Roseanna, Phoebe, Alexandra and David
Bedford, and Stuart Sweeney all fulfilled their role as
supermodels with aplomb. Thanks are also due to superstar
butcher's Levett & Hill of Droitwich.

Contents

Introduction

Ever since the first caveman dropped his brontosaurus steak into the fire and retrieved it, only to find that it tasted better somewhat burnt than it did when raw, the barbecue has had a very special place in our affections. Set aside the somewhat bizarre folk myth that barbecuing is the branch of cookery that is best-suited to men. Set aside all those North American rituals – the aprons with jokey pictures of huge bosoms; the burning of rare woods to smoke the food; and the preparation of incandescent macho chilli sauces. While you're at it, you can dispense with the traditional English barbecue style of cooking typified by a sausage burnt black on the outside and pinkly raw in the middle. This book attempts to reclaim the joys of cooking on a live fire for people who enjoy cooking indoors. The recipes I have included are authentic, culled from more than a dozen different cuisines. Some of the dishes may be complex, but they all work when followed step by step and they are particularly suited to cooking on a barbecue or open fire. There are dishes to suit a children's birthday party; an impromptu picnic; a lazy Sunday afternoon; a family get-together; a posh dinner party. I hope that there's something to please everyone and anyone. You'll find recipes for poultry, beef, lamb, pork, fish, vegetable dishes, breads and salads. You'll also find the technical tips to make what looks difficult at first glance a great deal easier. Why should we allow the word 'barbecue' to become shorthand for 'badly cooked indigestible food'? Why should cooks using an open fire always end up with blackened faces and burnt fingers? Out with the dull and in with something more interesting. Let's reclaim the joys of the live fire for genuine cooks.

Charles Campion

The fire and the fuel

When you walk into a hardware store or garden centre, you have only to whisper that you are interested in buying a barbecue for the salesman's eyes to take on a happy glint. Barbecues are big business – there are long, glossy, coach-built gas grills that cost as much as a second-hand sports car; there are huge rotund barbecues with complicated air vents; and there are natty portable grills perfect for the beach or picnics. They all have one thing in common: they provide a controllable outdoor source of heat for people who want to cook. In short, they tame your fire for you. With such a diversity, and as you can build a fire to cook on almost anywhere and in almost anything (the wheelbarrow below right was particularly successful), it is only logical that the different barbecue setups all have their own strengths and weaknesses. Here are some thoughts about the most popular commercial barbecues.

The basic barbecue

All purpose-built barbecues share some common features: there's somewhere for the coals to burn, and that place will usually have controllable ventilation; there's a grill on which to cook the food; and there is some means of adjusting the distance between the food and the fire. Thereafter, they can be round, square, or rectangular; on tall or short legs; a tiny grill or a forty-gallon oil drum cut in half lengthways!

Kettle barbecues

These tend to be large and have a lid. The key strengths are... that they are large and that they have lids! The size is helpful, because you can arrange the coals to give a variety of cooking temperatures (banking the coals up on one side means a hot zone and a cooler zone). The lid enables you to barbecue in a smoky, oven-like environment and, by adjusting the air vents, cook large joints slowly.

Gas barbecues

A good proportion of people who buy brand-new gas barbecues to replace their elderly charcoal grills are absolutely delighted by the fact that they no longer have to go through what they see as the rather lengthy business of lighting the coals, managing the fire, and then waiting for that perfect glow before starting to cook. The appeal of gas barbecues lies in striking a match, waiting for just two minutes, and then cooking immediately. In most models, the gas is used to heat a tray of lava rocks that lies below the grill. That 'original and genuine smoky barbecue taste' comes when the juices from the food splash down onto the hot rocks, burn, and turn to smoke – which is very close to what happens on a charcoal grill. You do not need charcoal or wood to achieve a smoky taste.

Ocakbasi

The ocakbasi is the Turkish barbecue. It is a compact and portable fire-box. The small size can be a real advantage, as long skewers lie across the grill with the handles protruding and you can turn them with ease. This barbecue also has the advantage that it can be refuelled quickly by lifting off the grill, which means that smaller can be quicker. You can buy a no-frills ocakbasi at Turkish and Middle Eastern stores – they are gratifyingly cheap.

Tawa

The tawa is the Indian chef's equivalent of the ocakbasi. These barbecues are usually rectangular and narrow, and roughly the same dimensions as a window-box for flowers. The tawa is best for skewered food as the cook is able to 'bridge' the skewers across the coals. You can buy these grills in Asian shops, where they also sell stout skewers, each with a wooden handle, so that the cook can twiddle his or her kebabs as if playing a game of table football!

Hibachi

The most petit of all the commonly available grills, the hibachi is a Japanese table-top grill. It usually has some sort of racking arrangement so that you can position the grills at different heights above the coals, and the intense heat is well-suited to food arranged on small bamboo skewers.

The open fire

Given that an open fire is just that – open – it can present problems when it comes to regulating the heat. But for cooking at low temperatures, i.e. when the coals have subsided to ashes and glow, the open fire cannot be beaten; just add a suitable grill and some means of securing it above the fire.

Fuel

The most consistent, reliable and commonplace barbecue fuel is charcoal, but the word 'charcoal' is something of a catch-all, covering everything from old-fashioned lumpwood charcoal (heavy and in irregular pieces) to briquettes (small nuggets made from pressed carbon dust) and bagged charcoal that has been pre-soaked in wax for easy lighting. One simple rule is to pick up the bag of charcoal and feel how heavy it is – the best charcoal is made from hard wood that is allowed to smoulder in a kiln with a minimum of oxygen. The charcoal that remains will be dense and feel heavy. Light and insubstantial charcoal has often been made from softwoods – it doesn't last as long as the heavier variety and it does not burn as hot.

If you wish to cook over a natural wood fire, the rules are much the same as when laying your living-room fire in the fireplace. The sappy softwoods full of resin, such as pine and birch, are the worst option, spitting and giving off oil smoke. The traditional hard woods like oak, beech and ash burn well and slowly, but need to be good and dry. They are the second-best option. The best wood of all is fruit wood (apple, pear, cherry), which is close-grained and slow-burning with an almost aromatic smoke.

Smoke

In America, barbecue cooks are unduly obsessive about smoke. This smoke often comes from wood chips that have been pre-soaked in water, then spread onto the coals and allowed to smoulder – or from a small bottle of chemicals labelled 'liquid smoke'. Such flavours are closer to the bludgeon than the rapier, and furthermore the idea of paying more money per kilo for wood chips than you would spend on fine steak rankles badly. So ignore the charms of pre-packed hickory, maple or mesquite chips, and rely on the juices from the food falling into the fire and vaporizing to add that elusive smoky tang. If you must dabble with extra smoke, here are three easier and cheaper options.

Seaweed – damp seaweed placed onto hot coals will liberate clouds of smoke with a not unpleasant whiff of iodine to add flavour.

Nut shells – save old walnut shells and soak in water. When sprinkled onto a hot fire, they will produce plenty of light-flavoured smoke.

Rosemary twigs – a bunch of rosemary twigs (pre-soaked in water) will make fragrant smoke when laid onto the coals. This also works with other woody herbs.

Lighting fires

The same salesman that is keen to sell you a super-whizzy de luxe barbecue will also be keen that you buy one of a huge range of different gadgets and potions for fire lighting. They all work, but few as well as the simplest: the chimney. You can even make this 'barbecue starter' for yourself as the construction is very simple. You need a light metal cylinder about 30cm in diameter and about 75cm deep. That's it. Start by stacking your coals in the chimney and lighting the fuel at the bottom – commercially made starters have draught holes at the base. The chimney will draw the flames up through the charcoal, and after five minutes you simply lift the collar-like chimney up and away to scatter the glowing coals in the barbecue fire-box.

However you manage to get the coals alight, there is almost an inevitability about the unwritten first law of barbecuing: 'the coals are always in perfect condition to start cooking just as you lift the last charred offering from the grill'. Be patient if you can.

There are special temperature gauges to let you know just how your barbecue is performing, but, as a more practical guide, here is a way to tell how things are going. Wait until the coals are a uniform ash grey. Remove the grid from your barbecue and put your hand over the coals at exactly the same height as the food would be.

- If the heat is uncomfortable after 2 seconds, the fire is 'Hot' and is hot enough to sear meat.
- If you can stand the heat for 3 or 4 seconds, the coals are 'Medium Hot' and the right heat for grilling.
- If you can stand the heat for 5 seconds, the coals are 'Medium to Slow' and perfect for cooking.

Sssh! Some secrets

- Get yourself the longest pair of spring-loaded tongs you can find – the best are those designed with scalloped jaws that seem to be favoured by chefs everywhere.

- The cut face of an onion is very useful, and very effective, for cleaning down the bars of a grill. Simply rub it over the grime.

- Always cover a barbecue that is to be left out in the open. If you let the ashes in your barbecue mix with rainwater, you end up with a liquid so corrosive that it will eat the bottom out of the most stalwart and most expensive piece of kit.

- If the fat and oil dripping from your food onto the coals makes cooking conditions too fierce, put an aluminium fast-food container containing 2cm of water on top of the coals and under the food. It will deflect the heat from underneath and keep the juices out of direct contact with the fire, thereby slowing down the flames and reducing the smoke.

- Mopping and sopping: there are special mops made for adding marinade to food on the grill. They make the job easier than when using a kitchen pastry brush, but probably qualify as an indulgence.

- Hand-held spritzers for spraying cut flowers are on sale at all good garden shops. Filled with water, these small plastic sprayers are very good for quelling fiery flare-ups and putting the brakes on the cooking process. Be sure that the one you use gives off a fine mist – any hint of 'squirt' will raise a plume of ash that can spoil your food.

- However strong the temptation, never add white spirit, lighter fuel, fire-lighters or other accelerants to a hot, or even a warm, fire. Burnt food is a waste; burnt people is a disaster.

- One of the most useful barbecue accessories is a table. The majority of cooks have a work-surface next to their kitchen cooker or hob, and barbecue chefs deserve to have the same amenities.

- A probe thermometer is the barbecue fanatic's friend and enables you to cut to the chase in those arguments about whether the a joint of meat is properly cooked. Insert the probe so that the tip is at the centre of the meat being tested and take the core temperature. Here's a guide:

  50°C/122°F   rare
  52°C/125°F   medium-rare
  57°C/134°F   medium
  65°C/149°F   medium-well
  70°C/158°F   well-done

- Do not overlook the merits of toast. Thick cut bread toasted over a hot fire, rubbed with the cut edge of a garlic clove and brushed with a little butter, is superb.

- Before grilling anything that is likely to stick to the bars (think fish), be sure to clean the grill thoroughly.

- When cooking anything, from chicken pieces to a whole fish, there is one absolutely foolproof method of telling when the food is cooked. Take it off the grill, cut it open with a knife and have a look!

- However basic your grill, remember that you can always invert a roasting tin over the food as it cooks to concentrate the heat. The proud owners of kettle barbecues simply bring their lids into play.

- When cooking over an open fire, remember that a peeled stick is not only hygienic but also disposable, and, if using green wood, a 'pre-soaked' skewer!

Sssh! Some secrets

Poultry

Whole chicken

Roast chicken, particularly a golden, spit-roast chicken, is such a rewarding dish that it would take a very arrogant cook to suggest any way of improving on it. However, let us suppose that you haven't got a mechanical spit handy and that you do not fancy standing turning the bird for over an hour. This recipe allows you to get a luxurious belt of flavour into your chicken and at the same time minimize dryness in the finished dish.

serves 4

1 bunch of fresh parsley	**2 tsp fine salt**
Green leafy bits of head of celery	**150g unsalted butter, warmed until very soft**
Freshly ground black pepper	**5 sprigs of tarragon, leaves stripped**
Juice of 1 lemon	**1 chicken, weighing 1.5–2kg**
⅛ tsp ground mace	**2 tbsp olive oil**

1 Assemble the herb butter. You can use a liquidizer or a pestle and mortar. With the liquidizer, add the parsley and celery leaves, then whizz. Add plenty of ground black pepper, the lemon juice, mace and salt and whizz again. Add the butter and the tarragon leaves and whizz until mixed. Pop in the refrigerator to firm and become manageable, about 30 minutes. For a pestle and mortar, chop the parsley and celery leaves in advance, then proceed as above. The butter will keep for a week or more.

2 To prepare the chicken, place it on a board with its back uppermost and the parson's nose pointing towards you. Take a stern pair of scissors and cut fore and aft along the back bone, running your scissors along one side of the parson's nose. Repeat on the opposite side and lift out the backbone. Flatten the chicken out, skin-side uppermost.

3 Use your hand to wriggle between the skin and flesh. Work the herb butter into this cavity, trying to cover the whole bird.

4 Oil the bird, get the coals medium-hot, and put a clean oiled rack 20cm over them. Start the bird with 4 minutes skin-side down to get the butter melted and the skin golden. Then turn it over and cook for about 30 minutes. The old test for a cooked chicken – the juices run clear when a skewer is plunged into the thickest point – works fine. The bird may need a last 3 minute burst skin-side down to brown it, and then it must rest for at least 15 minutes before serving.

- The dish will work indoors; just pop the chicken under a grill.
- This is a very good herb butter which works just as well with fish or pork.

- For an alternative butter with more zap, use coriander instead of parsley; 2 crushed garlic cloves; 1 tbsp hot curry paste, and the same amount of lemon juice, butter and seasoning.

Chicken wings in sweet black sauce

Everyone concedes that the tastiest meat lies closest to the bone, so the meat-to-bone ratio of a chicken wing is just about perfect. On the downside, they are fiddly to eat, but there is real finger-lickin' potential, so be sure to work on the sweet black sauce.

serves 6

4 tbsp black molasses	**3 tbsp cumin seeds**
Juice of 2 limes	**2 tbsp sea salt**
1 tbsp Worcestershire sauce	**1 tbsp freshly ground black pepper**
1 garlic clove, crushed	**24 chicken wings**
2 tsp fine salt	

1 Make the sweet black sauce by combining the molasses, lime juice, Worcestershire sauce, crushed garlic, and salt in a saucepan. Stir and bring to the boil. Remove from the heat and adjust to your taste (you may need more sweetness, more salt, more heat or more sharpness). Set aside – it is best served lukewarm.

2 Make the rub. Dry-roast the cumin seeds briefly in a frying pan to release their fragrance. Cool and mix with the salt and pepper. Liquidize and whizz to a sludge, or you can use a pestle and mortar.

3 Prepare the chicken wings and turn them into 'chicken lollipops' as they are called in India. Cut off the tips and save them for a worthy purpose such as making stock. Take the first joint and cut around the small end to sever the tendons, then scrape the meat back along the bone so that it forms a ball at the other end and you are left with the bone to use as a handle. Rub the cumin mix into all the chicken pieces and leave them covered in the refrigerator for 1 hour before cooking

4 You will need a medium heat, so lift the grill away from the coals. Oil a grill basket, or one of those devices that looks like a tennis racket. Add the chicken wings and cook for 5–7 minutes each side. Turn more frequently if they catch. Before serving, check they are cooked by lopping one wing in half with a knife – nothing should be pink!

5 To serve, either toss the wings in a bowl with the sweet black sauce or serve on plates with the sauce to one side.

⬤ This dish will work indoors; simply grill the wings. They make great, if rather messy, canapés.

⬤ The sweet black sauce is a firm favourite and will go with anything. It will keep for a week or so well-covered in the refrigerator.

Lemon and black pepper chicken

This is a dish so profoundly simple that it hardly looks worth bothering with, but I urge you to try it. The lemon juice firms up the chicken and helps keep it juicy.

serves 6

6 large chicken breasts, skin on

Juice of 3 lemons

2 tbsp freshly ground black pepper

2 tsp celery salt

1 Take the chicken breasts and make a series of shallow cuts, about 2.5mm, on the diagonal and about 2cm apart.

2 Mix the lemon juice and pepper together and rub into the chicken. Place on a large, flat dish, cover with cling film and leave in the refrigerator overnight (if you are pushed for time, a 4-hour marinade is the minimum).

3 Grill the chicken over a moderate barbecue. Start the meat with the skin side down and leave for about 5–8 minutes, then turn and keep a watchful eye in case it burns. It will take a further 8–10 minutes. The most accurate way to tell if the chicken is done is to remove a breast from the grill and cut it in half, nothing should be pink. Rest the chicken for 5 minutes somewhere warm before dusting with the celery salt and, if you are a fan, a little more freshly ground pepper.

- This recipe works well indoors. Just remember to grill the chicken pieces thoroughly and to rest them.

- This is a fashionable, minimalist dish that is at home in a dinner-party environment.

Bloody Mary chicken

As with all good marinades, this recipe aims to add both flavour and tenderness. It will work equally well with the white meat joints of a chicken, but choose the thighs for their meatiness and this marinade will help them along to tenderness. The alcoholic elements of the Bloody Mary may be omitted if you suddenly feel mean and decide that vodka should be reserved for drinking. The quantities below will make about 500ml of Bloody Mary – shaken or stirred, it's up to you.

serves 6

50ml dry sherry

75ml vodka

330ml tin of V8 vegetable juice

   (or use plain tomato juice and increase the celery salt to 2 tsp)

1 tbsp hot horseradish sauce

1 tsp celery salt

Juice of half a lemon

12 chicken thighs, on the bone

1 Mix together the sherry, vodka, vegetable juice, horseradish sauce, celery salt, and lemon juice. Roll the chicken thighs in the Bloody Mary mixture, cover the dish with cling film and leave in the refrigerator overnight (if you are pushed for time, a 4-hour soak is the minimum).

2 Grill the chicken pieces over a gentle barbecue – that point when the coals go very grey and the flames are just a memory is perfect. Start the meat with the skin-side down and leave for about 5–8 minutes, then turn and keep a watchful eye in case they burn. They will take a further 8–10 minutes. Test if it is cooked by cutting a thigh in half; there should be no sign of pink. Rest the meat for 5 minutes somewhere warm before eating.

- Good as finger food, needs little more accompaniment than crusty bread (pages 136 and 138) and salad (pages 141–146).
- This recipe works well indoors. Just remember to grill the chicken pieces as gently as you can, and then rest them.
- You can also use the Bloody Mary marinade for pork.

- You can make your own red sauce by reducing the remaining marinade in a saucepan until syrupy. Adjust the seasoning and add a dollop of honey. Hot-heads may wish to add a splash of chilli sauce.

Bloody Mary chicken with butterflied leg of lamb (page 61) and spring onions

Nonya poussin

Straits Chinese cuisine is starting to receive some recognition and is well-known for its vibrant flavours and no-nonsense attitudes. It combines elements from Chinese, Malay and Thai cooking. Nonya translates as 'matriarch' in the Hokkien dialect used by the Straits Chinese. This recipe is charming and practical – the majority of the preparation and cooking can be done ahead of time.

serves 6

6 spatchcocked poussins	**2 tbsp rice wine vinegar**
(a.k.a. spring chicken weighing	**8 cloves**
approximately 500g)	**3 tbsp runny honey**
100g muscovado sugar	**2 tsp fine salt**
75ml light soy sauce	**2 tsp five-spice powder**
75ml dark soy sauce	**1 cinnamon quill**
3 tbsp dry sherry	**1 tbsp sesame oil**

1 If you have been unable to persuade your butcher to do it for you, spatchcock the poussin by cutting along the backbone on each side, discarding it, and opening out the little chicken until it is flat.

2 Take your largest saucepan and add all the ingredients (except the chickens and oil) with 600ml of water and mix well. Then add the chickens. Transfer to the refrigerator, cover with cling film and leave to marinate for 2 hours.

3 Remove the chickens and set to one side. Bring the marinade to the boil and cook for 10 minutes. Return the chickens to the pot with the marinade, cover and boil for 10 minutes. Drain the chickens and allow to dry off before grilling.

4 Before cooking, paint the chickens with a little sesame oil. Over a moderate fire, start the chickens with 6–7 minutes with the breast-side uppermost. Finish with 5–6 minutes on the breast-side. They are ready when a poussin cut in half reveals no pink.

· ·

- This dish will work indoors, and as an alternative to grilling it is possible to deep-fry the poussin in the final stages.

- Poussin is for eating by hand, so if that is the way your dinner parties develop this dish could be a star turn.

Chicken satay

This is a classic restaurant dish and one that is built around the universal and ever-lasting appeal of the peanut. Just as with many sweetish sauces, it is up to the chef to decide just how far he or she indulges the diner's sweet tooth. Always balance sauces such as these to taste before serving.

serves 6

6 garlic cloves

Juice of 4 limes

100ml light soy sauce

750g chicken thigh or breast
   meat, cut into 1.5cm cubes

300g shallots, finely chopped

2 lemon grass stalks,
   finely chopped

1 tbsp hot chilli sauce

100ml groundnut oil

300g jar of crunchy peanut butter

1 tbsp fine salt

4 tbsp runny honey

1 Crush one of the garlic cloves and mix with the juice of two limes and the soy sauce in a flat dish and jumble the cubes of chicken in this marinade. Cover and set aside in the refrigerator for at least 4 hours and up to 12.

2 To make the satay sauce, place the shallots, remaining garlic cloves, lemon grass, and hot chilli sauce in a liquidizer and whizz to a paste. (Alternatively, pre-chop as necessary and use a pestle and mortar).

3 Heat the oil in a heavy frying pan and fry the paste – the flavours should be liberated but the paste must not end up looking too brown.

4 Transfer the paste to a large pan and add 1 litre of water, the peanut butter, salt, remaining lime juice, and the honey. Mix well, bring to the boil, and cook for about 10 minutes, longer if you find the texture too runny. Cool and set to one side. Adjust the seasoning in every dimension – sweetness, saltiness, sharpness, chilli heat.

5 Thread the cubed chicken onto small, pre-soaked bamboo skewers. Cook the skewers over a moderate grill, turning frequently. They should take 5–7 minutes. When checking if they are done, there is no substitute for cutting a piece of chicken open and studying the middle; no pink is good! Serve with the lukewarm satay sauce.

- This dish will work indoors; just use a grill.
- Satay sauce is always a winner and it will go with almost anything you care to grill.

- There is a version of this dish that is more pineappley and made with lamb on page 70.

Teriyaki chicken

This is a classic Japanese dish which revolves around a sweet/salty/savoury marinade that doubles up as a sauce. You should use fine bamboo skewers, but they need a good soak first for at least 2 hours or they will burn. And remember that when they come to the table, each skewer should look neat and dainty. Be sure to use a Japanese soy, and genuine mirin, which is a sweet varietal of sake.

serves 6

3 large chicken breasts, skinned	**75ml mirin**
75ml Japanese soy sauce	**1 tbsp runny honey**
75ml ordinary sake (or use dry sherry)	**¼ tsp cayenne pepper**
	Sea salt

1 Cut the chicken breasts into 2cm cubes – try and make them as neat and uniform as you can. Bring a pan of water to the boil, put the chicken pieces into a sieve, and plunge them into the boiling water for 30 seconds. Remove and rinse immediately under the cold tap. This will firm up the chicken pieces.

2 Thread the chicken pieces onto 18 pre-soaked bamboo skewers. Each piece should not touch its neighbour.

3 Make up the marinade by mixing 50ml of the Japanese soy sauce with 50ml of sake, 50ml of mirin, the honey, and the cayenne pepper. Reserve the rest to make the sauce.

4 Pour half the marinade into a flat dish and twirl the skewered chicken in it until coated. Arrange the skewers in the dish and pour over the remaining marinade. Cover with cling film and leave to marinate in the refrigerator for 30 minutes.

5 Make the sauce by draining the marinade into a saucepan and adding the remaining soy, sake, and mirin. Cook fiercely until all is reduced to a sticky sauce.

6 Cook the skewers over hot coals in small batches, turning constantly. Because the chicken pieces are small, they will only take 2–3 minutes. Check if they are done by splitting a piece with a knife – there should be no pink.

7 When all the skewers have been grilled, season with sea salt and pour the sticky sauce over them. Rest for 2 minutes before serving.

- This dish will work indoors, but you need a hot grill.

- There is no dishonour in using a commercial bottled teriyaki sauce. Just experiment until you find one that is to your taste.

Crispy chicken skin

Whenever you start that new and 'ultimate' slimming diet, you get given a list of things to do and things to avoid. It's a sucker bet that not eating the chicken skin is on almost every list of things to avoid. Skinless chicken pieces equal good; chicken pieces with skin equal bad. There is a reason for this: the skin of the chicken is the fattiest bit (bad), but the fat is what makes the flavour (good). So ignore the slimming diet, concentrate on dinner. These little skewers may be self-indulgent, but they are also very good.

serves 6

Plenty of chicken skin (this will depend on how many
chickens you are serving in other dishes!)
2 tbsp white-wine vinegar
1 tbsp olive oil
Sea salt and freshly ground black pepper

1 Cut the chicken skin into strips about 1cm by 5cm, or as best you can. Place them flat in a dish skin-side up and rub with the vinegar. Leave for 10 minutes.
2 Dry off with kitchen paper and oil the skin. Thread the skin onto small, pre-soaked bamboo skewers in a series of S-shaped pieces.
3 Cook over hot coals until crisp and golden, turning continually, about 3–4 minutes. Season with salt and pepper and serve.

• You can do this indoors under the grill, but it's a lot of work for an albeit delicious nibble.

Reshmi chicken kebabs

In Europe we don't make many dishes that call for minced chicken, perhaps because the glory of mince comes in the balance between lean meat and fat, and chicken meat is very lean indeed. The reshmi kebab is a Moghul invention that is very sophisticated and delicately spiced. To cook, mould the mixture around those flat, Turkish-style skewers that make turning kebabs so much easier.

serves 6

10g fresh root ginger, peeled and sliced

1 garlic clove

1 small green chilli, deseeded

600g finely minced chicken

150g curd cheese

1 tsp ground cardamom

½ bunch of fresh coriander leaves, finely chopped

1 tsp fine salt

Freshly ground black pepper

2 tbsp unsalted butter, melted

1 Pound the ginger and garlic in a pestle and mortar along with the chilli and a splash of water until you have a smooth paste.

2 Add this paste to the chicken in a mixing bowl. Add the cheese, cardamom, coriander, salt, and a few twists of black pepper. Mix thoroughly by hand.

3 Divide the mixture into 12. Wet your hands and mould each portion onto a flat skewer in the shape of a long cylinder. Each kebab should be no more than 2cm in diameter overall and about 8cm long.

4 Cook over hot coals for 4–5 minutes, turning frequently. Remove and rest the kebabs over a tray for 2–3 minutes to allow the excess moisture to drain away.

5 Brush the kebabs with melted butter and cook for a second time, about 2–3 minutes, until they take on a light golden colour. Make sure that the kebabs are done by cutting one in half and checking that it is not pink.

This dish will work indoors; the first stage of cooking in a hot oven (200°C/400°F/gas mark 6) and the second stage under a grill.

This makes a great starter, or serve it as part of a kebab feast together with the green chicken kebabs (page 30), methi chicken kebabs (page 31) and mughlai lamb tikka (page 67).

Jeera chicken

A favourite dish in sophisticated Indian restaurants, jeera chicken is a single-minded dish and so should you be! If you like cumin, this is the chicken for you. In restaurants, this dish would be cooked in a tandoori oven and tandoors deliver spectacularly high temperatures. So to cook this at home, you need the barbecue as hot as possible.

serves 6

100g fresh root ginger, finely grated

4 garlic cloves

1 large onion, finely chopped

3 tbsp groundnut oil

2 tbsp jeera (cumin seeds)

1 tsp coriander seeds

200ml plain yoghurt

¼ tsp mild chilli powder

1 tsp fine salt

6 large whole chicken legs (drumstick and thigh)

2 tbsp unsalted butter, melted

1 Put the ginger, garlic, onion, and 2 tbsp of groundnut oil into a liquidizer and whizz to a sludge, or you can use a pestle and mortar.

2 Dry-roast the cumin and coriander seeds in a frying pan to release their fragrance. Put 2 tsp of the roasted seeds aside for the final stage. Combine the onion paste with the roasted seeds, yoghurt, chilli powder, and salt to make the marinade.

3 Take each chicken leg and slash all over with a sharp knife – the cuts should be about 3cm apart and penetrate the flesh to a depth of about 5mm. Rub with the marinade and put them, together with any remaining marinade, into a strong plastic bag. Expel the air, seal, and leave in the refrigerator to marinate for 6 hours.

4 To cook, get the coals of the barbecue grey/white – you want it as hot as possible. Oil the skewers before use and allow two parallel skewers per chicken leg so that they are easy to turn on the grill. Grill for about 5 minutes each side, but turn more frequently if they start to burn. Baste with melted butter using a pastry brush. Rest the skewers away from the fire for 10 minutes.

5 Finally, cook for another 5 minutes each side, basting with melted butter, before resting for a further 10 minutes. Make sure they are done by cutting one in half and making sure it is not pink. Baste one last time just before serving and sprinkle with the roasted seeds that you have put by.

• This dish will work indoors; get your oven as hot as you can (200°C/400°F/gas 6) and prepare for a smoky kitchen.

• Accompany your jeera chicken with flat breads (page 135) and a crisp salad (page 142).

Green chicken kebabs

These green chicken kebabs feature on the menu at a number of very chic Indian restaurants (in such places it is sometimes called chicken hariyali). The two main foundations of the recipe are an implausible amount of green herbs and thick yoghurt. They look very good and taste even better.

serves 6

75g fresh root ginger

6 garlic cloves

Juice of half a lemon

20ml vegetable oil

1 tsp freshly ground black pepper

2 tsp fine salt

12 boneless chicken thighs, skinned

1 large bunch of fresh mint

1 large bunch of fresh coriander (it's hard to have too much green stuff!)

100g frozen spinach, thawed

4 green chillies, deseeded and finely chopped

30ml mustard oil

150ml thick yoghurt

1 tsp garam masala

2 tbsp unsalted butter, melted

1 Using a liquidizer (or a pestle and mortar), whizz the ginger and garlic with a splash of water to make a paste. Leave half the paste in the liquidizer. Transfer the remainder to a shallow bowl and add the lemon juice, oil, black pepper, and salt.

2 Cut each chicken thigh into three equal chunks. Rub the ginger marinade into the chicken pieces, then cover and leave in the refrigerator for 1 hour.

3 Now make the green marinade. Add the mint, coriander, spinach and chilli to the remaining paste. Whisk in the mustard oil, yoghurt and garam masala.

4 Add the chicken with ginger marinade to the green marinade. Rub in well, cover, and leave for a further 1 hour. Skewer the chicken – six pieces to a long metal skewer.

5 To cook, get the coals of the barbecue grey/white, as hot as possible. Grill for about 3 minutes each side, but turn more often if they start to burn. Baste sparingly with melted butter using a pastry brush. Rest the skewers away from the fire for 10 minutes.

6 Finally, cook for another 3 minutes each side, basting sparingly with melted butter, before resting for a further 5 minutes and serving. Make sure that the kebabs are done by cutting one in half and checking that it is not pink.

· ·

- This dish will work indoors; get your oven as hot as you can (200°C/400°F/gas mark 6) and prepare for a smoky kitchen.

- This goes well as part of a kebab feast, with the reshmi chicken kebabs (page 27), methi chicken kebabs (page 31), and mughlai lamb tikka (page 67).

Methi chicken kebabs

The taste of methi, which we know as fenugreek, is one of those 'love it' or 'hate it' deals. If you like it, this dish will be delightful; if not, best to give methi kebabs a miss. To cook them, mould the mixture around those flat, Turkish-style skewers that make turning kebabs so much easier.

serves 6

30ml mustard oil

1 tsp cumin seeds

1 garlic clove, crushed

200g fresh methi leaves
   (fenugreek), finely chopped

600g finely minced chicken

50g curd cheese

1 medium onion, finely chopped

1 egg yolk

1 tsp hot chilli powder

1 tsp fine salt

2 tsp allspice

2 tsp ground fenugreek

1 tsp garam masala

2 tbsp unsalted butter, melted

1 Heat the mustard oil in a frying pan – ensure that it is hot enough to smoke as this will temper its fierceness. Reduce the heat and fry the cumin seeds until they crackle, then add the garlic and fenugreek leaves and wilt. Allow to cool.

2 Put the chicken mince into a bowl and add the fenugreek mix from the frying pan. Mix thoroughly with the other ingredients: curd cheese, onion, egg yolk, chilli powder, salt, allspice, ground fenugreek, and garam masala.

3 Divide the mixture into 12. Wet your hands and mould each portion onto a flat skewer in the shape of a long cylinder. Each kebab should be no more than 2cm in diameter and about 8cm long.

4 Cook over hot coals for 4–5 minutes, turning frequently. Remove and rest the kebabs over a tray for 2–3 minutes to allow the excess moisture to drain away.

5 Brush the kebabs with melted butter and cook for a second time, about 2–3 minutes, until a light-golden colour. Make sure that the kebabs are done by cutting one in half and checking that it is not pink.

- This dish will work indoors; simply cook under a grill.

- This makes a great starter, or serve it as part of a kebab feast together with the reshmi chicken kebabs (page 27), green chicken kebabs (page 30), and mughlai lamb tikka (page 67).

Chicken tikka

Chicken tikkas are small, roughly 3cm by 3cm cubes of boneless chicken cut from either the breast or leg – the small size of the cubes means that they cook quickly and evenly. This recipe adds an extravagant and very delicious whiff of saffron, which makes it a good deal more sophisticated than the chicken tikka at your local Indian restaurant. Also note that there is no artificial colouring.

serves 6

¼ tsp saffron strands

8 green cardamom pods

½ large fresh papaya,
   or two small ones

200ml plain yoghurt

3 tbsp groundnut oil

2 tsp fine salt

1kg boneless chicken, cut into tikkas

2 tbsp unsalted butter, melted

1 Put the saffron into an egg cup and add a splash of boiling water. Leave to infuse.
2 Put the cardamom pods into a liquidizer and whizz them dry until they become a fine powder. You can also make the marinade with a pestle, mortar and a little elbow grease, if you prefer.
3 Discard the papaya seeds, then scoop out the flesh and add it to the liquidizer with the yoghurt, oil and salt. Whizz it, then add the saffron and its water and whizz again.
4 Rub the tikkas with this marinade and put them, together with any remaining marinade, in a strong plastic bag. Expel the air and leave in the refrigerator to marinate for 6 hours.
5 Oil long metal skewers lightly before use, then skewer the tikkas onto them (or bamboo skewers that have been soaked in water for at least two hours). Do not allow the cubes of meat to touch – when pressed together tightly they don't cook so well.
6 To cook, get the coals of the barbecue grey/white; as hot as possible. Grill for about 3 minutes each side, but turn more often if they start to burn. Baste sparingly with melted butter using a pastry brush. Rest the skewers away from the fire for 10 minutes.
7 Finally, cook for another 3 minutes each side, basting sparingly with melted butter, before resting for a further 5 minutes and serving. Make sure that the tikkas are done by cutting one in half and checking that it is not pink.

- This dish will work indoors; get your oven as hot as you can (200°C/400°F/gas mark 6) and prepare for a smoky kitchen.

- To make a sauce, cook the remaining marinade gently in a pan until thick and sticky. Stir in 100g of finely chopped roasted cashew nuts. Adjust the seasoning and serve.

Malai chicken tikka

This chicken tikka has an initial marinade to tenderize the meat, then a second marinade that clings to the cubes and forms a creamy-cheey coat. Cooking these tikkas is a delicate business, as you want the meat cooked through but the coating smoky.

serves 6

8 green cardamom pods

1 tsp freshly ground black
pepper

4 tbsp groundnut oil

2 tsp fine salt

¼ a ripe pineapple, peeled and
chopped

1kg chicken, cut into tikkas

50g fresh root ginger

1 garlic clove

5 hot green chillies, deseeded

60ml double cream

120ml plain yoghurt

50g cream cheese

1 tbsp cornflour

1 bunch of green coriander, finely chopped

1 Using a liquidizer, whizz the cardamom pods dry until they become a fine powder. Add the pepper, 3 tbsp of the oil, the salt and pineapple and whizz all together.

2 Rub the tikkas with the marinade and put them, together with the marinade, into a strong plastic bag. Expel the air and marinate in the refrigerator for 30 minutes.

3 To make the coating marinade, whizz the ginger with the garlic and chillies. Beat the cream, yoghurt and cheese together in a bowl. Combine the cornflour with a little water and work it into the mix. Add the ginger mixture and coriander and combine.

4 Oil long metal skewers lightly before use, then skewer the tikkas. Do not allow the cubes of meat to touch. Lay the skewers out on a dish and pour over the creamy marinade. Coat well, cover, and leave in the refrigerator for 6 hours. 15 minutes before cooking, pop the tikkas in the freezer to set the creamy coating on the outside.

5 To cook, get the barbecue coals grey/white – you want it as hot as possible. Grill for about 3 minutes each side, but turn more often if they start to burn. Baste sparingly with oil using a pastry brush. Rest the skewers away from the fire for 10 minutes.

6 Cook for another 3 minutes each side, basting sparingly with oil, before resting for 5 minutes and serving. Test by cutting one tikka in half; there should be no pink.

This dish will work indoors; get your oven as hot as you can (200°C/400°F/gas mark 6) and prepare for a smoky kitchen.

To make a sauce, cook the remaining marinade gently in a pan until thick and sticky. Stir in 100g of finely chopped roasted cashew nuts. Adjust the seasoning and serve.

Chilli chicken thighs

Every now and then we all crave something hot – perhaps a belt of chilli hot enough to make the eyes water. Around the world, a host of Indian, Mexican and Caribbean restaurants are happy co-conspirators in our quest for the burn. As it stands, even a hardened chilli head would find this dish hot, but you can make it milder if you wish – simply reduce the number of chillies.

serves 6

100g fresh root ginger, finely grated

4 garlic cloves

1 large onion, finely chopped

4 small, hot red chillies

3 tbsp groundnut oil

1 tbsp amchoor (sour mango powder)

2 tsp fine salt

12 large chicken thighs, skinned but on the bone

2 tbsp unsalted butter, melted

1 Put the ginger, garlic, onion, and chillies (including the seeds if you like really hot food) plus the groundnut oil into a liquidizer and whizz to a sludge. Alternatively, use a pestle, mortar and hard work!

2 Add the amchoor and salt and whizz some more, until thoroughly mixed.

3 Take each chicken thigh and slash it all over with a sharp knife – the cuts should be about 3cm apart and penetrate the flesh to a depth of about 5mm. Either wear gloves for the next procedure or wash your hands very carefully afterwards – chilli will burn any areas of sensitive skin. Rub the chicken thighs with the marinade and put them, together with any remaining marinade, into a strong plastic bag. Expel the air and leave the bag in the refrigerator to marinate for between 2 and 6 hours – the longer the time, the hotter things will get.

4 To cook, get the coals of the barbecue grey/white – you want the grill as hot as possible. Oil eight thin skewers before use and thread three thighs onto each pair of skewers so that they are easy to turn on the grill. Grill for about 6 minutes each side, but turn more frequently if they start to burn. Baste with melted butter using a pastry brush. Rest the skewers away from the fire for 10 minutes.

5 Cook for another 5 minutes each side, basting with melted butter, before resting for 10 minutes. Test if they are done by cutting one thigh in half; there should be no pink.

· This dish will work indoors; get your oven as hot as you can (200°C/400°F/gas mark 6) and prepare for a smoky kitchen.

· The burning component in chilli is capsaicin. As it is only soluble in fat, the one drink that helps alleviate a burn is milk or yoghurt. A chilli burn only lasts for 10 minutes.

Jerk chicken

Some say that this Caribbean favourite got its name from the word 'jook', which means poking meat with a sharp, pointed stick to help flavours reach the centre. Or perhaps it derives from the preservative effects of this salty, spicy paste – along the lines of beef jerky. Either way, it has become barbecue shorthand for maximum chilli with a belt of another Caribbean flavour, allspice. Not for the faint-hearted.

serves 6

6 whole habenero chillies (you can cut this back to 2, and deseed them, if nervous)
3 medium onions, chopped
150g spring onions, chopped, including the green parts
4 garlic cloves, crushed
1 bunch of fresh parsley, chopped
1 bunch of fresh coriander, chopped

2 tbsp muscovado sugar
2 tsp fine salt
1 tbsp allspice
1 tbsp mixed spice
1 tbsp dried thyme leaves
Juice of 3 limes
2 tbsp dark soy sauce
2 tbsp vegetable oil
6 large whole chicken legs
2 tbsp unsalted butter, melted

1 Whizz the chillies, onions, spring onions, garlic, and soft herbs in a liquidizer to a stiff paste. Sprinkle in the sugar, salt, allspice, mixed spice, and thyme and whizz again.
2 Leave the motor running and gradually add the lime juice, soy sauce and oil. Finally, add enough water to create a thick, spreadable paste.
3 Take each chicken leg and slash all over with a sharp knife – the cuts should be about 3cm apart and penetrate the flesh to a depth of about 5mm. Rub with the jerk paste (use gloves, or wash very carefully – chilli is painful stuff especially on tender skin or if it gets in the eyes), then put the chicken legs into a strong plastic bag, expel the air and leave in the refrigerator to marinate for 6 hours.
4 To cook, get the coals of the barbecue grey/white – you want it as hot as possible. Oil the skewers before use and allow two parallel skewers per chicken leg so that they are easy to turn on the grill. Grill for about 5 minutes each side, but turn more frequently if they start to burn. Rest the skewers away from the fire for 10 minutes.
5 Cook for another 5 minutes on each side, basting with melted butter, before resting for 10 minutes. Use a knife to cut one piece deeply; it's done when there is no pink.

- The jerk rub will keep tightly sealed in the refrigerator for a couple of weeks.
- You can use the jerk rub to 'jerk' anything: steaks, chops, fish.

Rosemary chicken livers

Simple but delicious, this quick and easy dish makes a grand starter or nibble. Skewering the livers is difficult, but it's made easier if you choose large, perky livers.

serves 6

150ml port	2 x 250g tubs of chicken livers
2 garlic cloves, crushed	12 long, woody rosemary twigs
Sea salt and ground black pepper	1 tbsp unsalted butter, melted

1 Mix the port and garlic in a bowl, and add a couple of twists of black pepper. Pick over the livers and select the largest and firmest. Add them to the port, cover, and put aside in the refrigerator to marinate for anything between 12 and 18 hours.

2 Strip the leaves from your rosemary twigs leaving a tuft at the end. Scatter them over the coals to add scented smoke.

3 When ready to cook, skewer the livers and rest them on a piece of kitchen foil. Place the entire foil sheet over gentle coals and cook for 6-7 minutes, turning often – put a doubled sheet of foil under the bushy ends so they don't burn. When cooked, the livers should be pink in the middle. Brush with melted butter, season with salt, and serve.

Blackcurrant pigeon breast

Some town dwellers call pigeons 'flying rats', and it is hard to make a case for the grizzled urban pigeons of Trafalgar Square making a decent meal. But a sleek, plump bird fresh from its onslaught on a farmer's field is great eating – just use the breasts and forget the carcasses. Thank goodness pigeons are so cheap.

serves 6

100ml balsamic vinegar

150ml cassis (blackcurrant liqueur)

1 tbsp Worcestershire sauce

12 pigeon breasts, skinned

Sea salt

1 Mix together the balsamic vinegar, cassis and Worcestershire sauce.

2 Turn the pigeon breasts over in the marinade, then put them in a bowl, covering them with the marinade. Cover with cling film and put in the refrigerator for 24 hours minimum, up to 72 hours. The action of the acid and alcohol in the marinade will all but 'cook' the meat – it's the same process for making an escabeche with fish.

3 Remove the pigeon pieces, by now smaller and firmer. You need a grill of moderate heat and, following such a long marination, the pigeon will cook very quickly – 2 minutes each side. You're aiming for a very juicy, underdone interior and a crisp exterior. Cut one and check, if you are nervous. Salt them as they come off the grill.

● This dish will work indoors; just use a hot grill and garnished with a few sprigs of fresh blackcurrants (if they are in season), it makes a good dinner-party dish.

Honeyed duck magret

Magret de canard is quite tricky to cook, mainly because you must first achieve a consensus among your diners as to how well done it should be served. Some folk like their duck breasts red, raw and bleeding and others veer towards the grey and solid. Here is a basic duck recipe that should please everybody. Remember that the pre-packed duck breasts vary in size from 160g tiddlers to 350g barbary duck monsters, so one solution is to give the people who want their duck well done a small one and the rare fraternity one of the larger ones.

serves 6

50ml cider vinegar

6 duck breasts

75g unsalted butter

100ml runny honey

2 tsp fine salt

1 Pour the cider vinegar into a flat dish. Add the duck breasts skin-side down and leave covered in the refrigerator for 30 minutes.

2 Remove the duck and dry it carefully with some kitchen paper. Prick the skin side all over with a fork.

3 To grill, start with moderate coals and put a foil drip tray on top of the coals under the area of the grill that you will be using. Start by grilling the breasts for 4–5 minutes skin-side down, then turn and give them a further 4–5 minutes. Take them off the fire and leave to rest for 10 minutes before serving. Given the variabilities of barbecues, there is no substitute for cutting a duck breast in half to check that it is cooked to your liking.

4 Melt the butter in a saucepan, then add the honey and salt, and stir. Arrange the duck breasts skin-side up and pour the honey butter over them.

This dish will work indoors; just use a hot grill, and settle the likes and dislikes of your guests.

Quail's egg skewers

This recipe was developed after a trip to a Japanese restaurant in North London, where the chef produced some immaculate little skewers with winning combinations of ingredients. Celery salt, the traditional accompaniment to larger gull's eggs, works very well at the end.

serves 6

18 quail's eggs

6 asparagus spears, chopped, or chunks of green pepper

2 tbsp mirin

Celery salt

1 Hard-boil the quail's eggs for 5 minutes, then plunge into iced water and peel.
2 Carefully thread the eggs onto skewers using the asparagus or peppers as spacers. Brush with mirin and cook gently over a dying barbecue for 3 minutes, turning occasionally. Just get the eggs hot through and leave the green stuff crunchy.
3 Before serving, brush with mirin and dust with celery salt.

Turkish quail

In those smoky Turkish grill houses called 'ocakbasi', the chef sits behind a trough of glowing coals and cooks everything from sweetbreads to lamb fillet. As well as amazing dexterity, his trade secrets include all manner of skewering techniques – how you arrange the meat on the skewers governs the speed of cooking. Quail may be tiny but they barbecue very well indeed. Sumac is a deep-red, dried herb that tastes lemony and spicy. You can get it in Middle Eastern stores.

serves 6

12 oven-ready quail

200ml olive oil

2 tbsp ground sumac

Juice of half a lemon

1 tbsp sea salt

2 tsp freshly ground back pepper

1 Take a knife and split the quails, cutting down through the breast. Flatten them out and tuck their wings in tidily.

2 Mix together the olive oil and sumac and work half the mixture into the quails. Arrange the birds in a flat dish and pour over the marinade. Cover with cling film and leave them in the refrigerator to marinate for 24 hours – 36 wouldn't hurt.

3 Take the quail out of the marinade and wipe off any excess oil. Lay each quail out flat and take two long skewers. Thread each pair of quail onto a pair of skewers – the dual skewer will hold the birds squarely and make them easy to turn.

4 Sprinkle the quail with lemon juice, then rub the salt and pepper into the birds and leave to dry off for 1 hour.

5 When the coals are giving out plenty of heat, grill the quail, skin-side down, for 4–5 minutes, until the skin is crispy. Turn them and cook more slowly (move to a cooler area of the coals) for a further 4–5 minutes. Allow the birds to rest and serve with the onion salad below. Test if they are done by cutting through the thickest part.

- This dish will work indoors, and you can use either a hot oven or a grill.
- You can substitute poussin for quail; just up the cooking times to 8–10 minutes a side and check carefully for 'doneness' before serving.

- The delicious onion salad is made by slicing sweet red onions, then jumbling them in your hands with 1 tbsp of sumac, 1 tsp of salt, and a good squeeze of lemon juice. Leave in a dish for 10 minutes to allow the flavours to mingle, then add another squeeze of lemon juice.

Beef

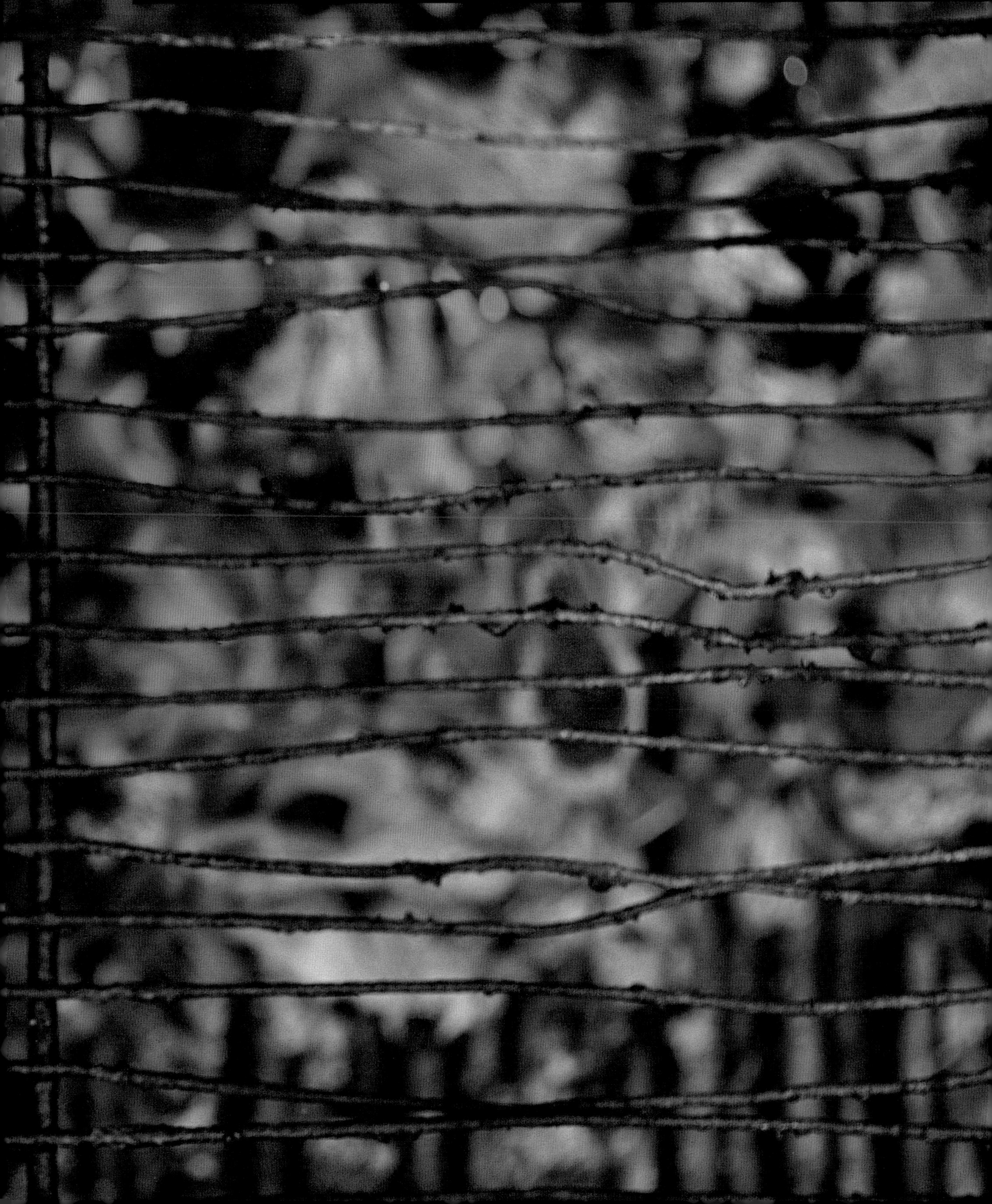

Hamburgers

Enough books have been written about hamburgers to stock a modest library, and the dish itself has been made using everything from fillet steak to chopped tuna – though, strangely, never ham! Eminent American food writer James Beard suggests placing an ice-cube at the heart of each burger so that the interior stays rare while the exterior ends up crisp and well-done. Mine is a simple recipe that will end up juicy and delicious – but if you don't like it, you can always experiment with grilling ice-cubes!

serves 6

1 large onion, finely chopped	**2 tsp sea salt**
2 tbsp unsalted butter	**Freshly ground black pepper**
1kg minced, lean rump steak	**2 tbsp double cream**

1 Soften the onion in the butter over a gentle heat, then add to the meat in a large bowl and sprinkle over the salt and a few twists of freshly ground black pepper

2 Add the double cream and mix all together gently – do not overwork the mix. Divide into 12 flat-ish hamburgers, cover, and put in the refrigerator to mature for an hour.

3 To cook, you will need a barbecue where the heat is between medium and hot. Give the burgers 3 minutes on the first side, getting a good seal that holds the burger together. Then turn and give them another 4–5 minutes if you like your hamburger rare; plus a further 2 minutes for well-done. Rest the burgers for 4 minutes.

● These hamburgers work perfectly indoors; either pan-fry or grill them.

● Serve the hamburgers with a green salad, or slip them into a soft, round bread roll. They go well with the barbecue sauce on page 147.

Guinness hamburgers

This is an implausible recipe, but there is something about the chemical interactions of fizzy liquid (in this case, Guinness) and the protein in lean meat that helps bind everything together. The faint bitterness of the stout also helps tenderize the meat and balance the flavours.

serves 6

1kg roughly minced, lean rump steak

6 spring onions, finely chopped, including the green parts

2 tbsp hot grain mustard

100ml Guinness

2 tsp sea salt

Freshly ground black pepper

1 Spread the meat out on a large dish and sprinkle the chopped onion over it. Distribute the mustard and splash the Guinness onto the meat, season, and bring everything together with a fork – do not overwork the mix. Divide into 12 flat-ish hamburgers, cover, and set aside in the refrigerator to mature for an hour.

2 To cook the hamburgers, you will need a barbecue where the heat is somewhere between medium and hot. Give them 3 minutes on the first side, being sure to get a good seal that will hold the burger together. Then turn and give them another 4–5 minutes, if you like your hamburger rare. For well-done, a further 2 minutes cooking is recommended. Rest the hamburgers for 4 minutes before serving.

- These hamburgers work perfectly indoors; either pan-fry or grill them.
- The vague sharpness of the Guinness means that these burgers work well with a slice of mild cheese as counterpoint.
- These hamburgers go well with the barbecue sauce on page 147.

Sirloin steaks with chimichurri

If there were to be a carnivores' Olympics, the Texans would go into the early heats confident of getting gold, until the moment they came up against the team from Argentina. Every 'parilla', or grill-house, in Argentina churns out huge portions of tender slabs of prime steak. How Argentines end up as lean, mean polo-playing pin-ups is a mystery. The key to a steak with Argentine appeal lies in the chimichurri, with its garlic (to give you bad breath) and parsley (to save you from bad breath).

serves 6

75ml distilled white vinegar

100ml olive oil

2 tsp freshly ground black pepper

2 tsp fine salt

1 tsp dried oregano

1 large bunch of parsley, very finely chopped

1 bunch of spring onions, very finely chopped, including the green parts

1 small green chilli, deseeded and finely chopped

6 garlic cloves, crushed

6 thick sirloin steaks, about 2cm thick

1 Make the chimichurri, which has two roles: a quarter of the quantity is used as a marinade/wet rub before the steaks are cooked, and the remainder becomes a sauce. Whisk the vinegar, oil, black pepper, salt, and oregano together in a jug until they emulsify and thicken. Add a splash of water to help them combine.

2 Stir the green stuff into the liquid with the garlic. Adjust the seasoning. The chimichurri only keeps for about 4 hours before the green colour begins to go khaki.

3 Trim away all but 1.5cm of the fat on the steaks. Rub with a quarter of the chimichurri, cover, and put in the refrigerator to marinate for about 30 minutes.

4 To cook, first get the coals very hot. Then start by searing the steaks on both sides as well as the edges. This should take about 1 minute a side.

5 Either raise the grill to reduce the heat, or use the fringes where the fire is less fierce to cook the steaks over a medium heat; about 4 minutes for one side plus 5–6 minutes on the second side for rare or as much as 8–9 minutes for well-done. (If you have a probe thermometer, a core temperature of 50°C indicates rare; 52°C medium-rare; 57°C medium; 65°C medium-well; and 70°C well-done. Otherwise, cut one open and take a look.)

6 Allow the meat to rest for at least 5 minutes. Serve your steaks with chimichurri.

- Indoor steaks are just fine; use your grill.
- For a sauce developed by the world's greatest steak-eaters, chimichurri works surprisingly well with fish dishes.

Spiced côte de boeuf

The côte de boeuf is the cut of meat that looks like a large, thick beef chop – cook it rare and slice it with the grain. This seasoning would also work well with the cut that butchers sell as ribeye (in practice, this is the meaty bit of the côte de boeuf). Ready-ground garam masala is widely available.

serves 6

1 garlic clove

3 thick (3cm) côte de boeuf, including the bone

500ml red wine

75ml olive oil

3 tsp green peppercorns

2 tsp garam masala

1 tbsp dried oregano

1 Cut the garlic clove in half and rub the meat all over with the cut ends before laying them out on a tray. Mix the wine and oil together and pour the liquid over the beef. Work it in with your fingers.

2 Grind the green peppercorns coarsely and sprinkle half of them over the steaks. Then dust with half the garam masala and half the oregano. Turn the meat over and repeat with the remainder of the spices. Cover the meat with some cling film and leave in the refrigerator for 4 hours.

3 To cook, first get the coals very hot. Then start by searing the meat on both sides as well as the edges. This should take about 1 minute a side.

4 Either raise the grill to reduce the heat, or use the fringes where the fire is less fierce to cook the steaks over a medium heat – about 4 minutes for the first side plus about 5–6 minutes on the second side for rare or as much as 8–9 minutes for well done. (If you have a probe thermometer, remember that a core temperature of 50°C indicates rare; 52°C medium-rare; 57°C medium; 65°C medium-well; and 70°C well-done. Otherwise, cut one open and take a look.)

5 Take the meat from the fire and allow to rest for at least 5 minutes. Cut the meat into slices, carving with the grain.

- Indoor steaks are just fine; use your grill.
- This marinade will work for any (relatively tender) cut of meat – rump steak, pork steak, even lamb.

Fillet steak with bacon and onion butter

Fillet steaks hold sway as the most expensive cut at most steak-houses. But whisper it: they are sometimes so tender and so delicate that they don't taste of much at all. It's our fault for clinging to the idea that what is most expensive is usually the best. This recipe takes a simply tender piece of meat and adds some rough flavours. Princely with a touch of peasant!

serves 6

6 rashers of fat streaky bacon

100g unsalted butter

1 large onion, very finely chopped

6 fillet steaks, 200–250g each

1 Make the butter a day in advance to allow it to chill well. Remove the bacon rinds and put the rashers on a rack in a roasting tin. Cook in a hot oven (200°C/400°F/gas mark 6) for 10 minutes, or until you have crispy bacon and a pool of delicious bacon fat. Break into small crisp shards.

2 Melt the butter in the bacon fat in the roasting tin, mix well, and stir in the onion and bacon. Let the mix become cool and malleable, then form into a roll on a double thickness of cling film. Roll carefully and twist the ends so that you end up with a cylinder about 3cm in diameter. Place in the refrigerator for 24 hours.

3 Remember to take your steaks out of the refrigerator a couple of hours before you want to cook them. Fillet steaks are thick, and there is nothing worse than a steak that remains fridge-cold at the centre.

4 Start by searing your steaks for 1 minute on each side over a hot fire. Then either raise the grill to reduce the heat, or use the fringes where the fire is less fierce to cook the steaks over a medium heat – about 4 minutes for the first side plus about 5–6 minutes on the second side for rare or as much as 8–9 minutes for well-done. (If you have a probe thermometer, remember that a core temperature of 50°C indicates rare; 52°C medium-rare; 57°C medium; 65°C medium-well; and 70°C well-done. Otherwise, cut one open and take a look.)

5 Slice through your roll of bacon and onion butter to give 1cm-thick medallions. Allow the meat to rest for at least 5 minutes while the butter melts over each steak.

- Indoor steaks are just fine; use your grill.   ● See also the chive butter on page 148.

Rump steak with monkey gland sauce

Monkey gland sauce is a South African invention, and thankfully has very little to do with either monkeys or glands! The Rainbow Nation is very fond of a 'brai' (barbecue), and this sauce is interesting in that, unlike so many barbecue favourites, it is not wildly hot. Instead, it is rather on the sweet side. You can use it as both a sauce and as a wet rub or marinade.

serves 6

75ml red wine	**1 tbsp fine salt**
75ml Coca-Cola	**200g sweet mango chutney**
75ml port	**75g cold butter, cubed**
1 tsp hot chilli sauce	**6 rump steaks, 350g each and 2cm thick**

1 To make the monkey gland sauce – something that is best accomplished a day or two ahead of time – put the wine, Coca-Cola, and port into a saucepan, bring to the boil and reduce by two-thirds, until you have 75ml of thick liquid. Add the chilli sauce and salt and mix together well.

2 Take the chutney and pour it out onto a plate. Chop up the large bits of mango with a knife, add it to the reduction and bring to the boil, stirring to bring everything together. Finally, whisk in the cold butter, which should emulsify your sauce. Allow to cool and keep in a covered jar in the refrigerator. This will keep for at least 10 days.

3 Take your steaks and trim away all but 1.5cm of the fat. Rub them with a couple of tablespoonfuls of the monkey gland sauce and put them into the refrigerator, covered, to marinate for about 30 minutes.

4 To cook, first get the coals very hot. Then start by searing the steaks on both sides as well as the edges. This should take about 1 minute a side.

5 Either raise the grill to reduce the heat, or use the fringes where the fire is less fierce to cook the steaks over a medium heat – about 4 minutes for the first side plus about 5–6 minutes on the second side for rare or as much as 8–9 minutes for well-done. (If you have a probe thermometer, remember that a core temperature of 50°C indicates rare; 52°C medium-rare; 57°C medium; 65°C medium-well; and 70°C well-done. Otherwise, cut one open and take a look.)

6 Allow the meat to rest for at least 5 minutes and serve with monkey gland sauce.

● For all but South Africans, monkey gland sauce can be too sweet, so you may wish to adjust the finished sauce with fresh lime juice.

Pineapple lamb shanks

Once upon a time lamb shanks (the knuckley bit from a shoulder of lamb or the shin section from the leg), were given away by butchers. But then they became a firm favourite with smart chefs and the price soared. Shanks go well on the barbecue, providing that you can cook them slowly enough. The large bone makes them rigid and the 'crispy bits' at the edges are especially good.

serves 6

1 pineapple

Juice of 1 lemon

1 tbsp molasses sugar

1 tbsp mild curry paste

6 lamb shanks

1 Take the pineapple – ideally an over-ripe one that has lain forgotten at the back of the fruit bowl until past its best – and peel carefully, then chop finely, saving the juice. Put it into a liquidizer or pestle and mortar along with the juice.

2 Add the lemon juice, sugar, and curry paste – any commercial kurma paste will do. It is simply used to add a faint exotic note. Whizz to a fine sludge.

3 Rub the marinade into the lamb shanks, and put the shanks and remaining marinade into a thick plastic bag. Expel the air, seal, and transfer to the refrigerator to marinate for at least 4 hours; 24 hours would be best.

4 To cook the shanks, either start them off with 45 minutes in a low oven (130°C/250°F/gas mark ½), or if you have a kettle barbecue turn it to minimum and cook them with the lid closed for 30 minutes.

5 For the final cooking, finish over glowing coals for 8–10 minutes, turning as necessary, but keep your wits about you as the high sugar content of the marinade means that the shanks will burn easily. Aim for plenty of crispy bits. Allow to rest and cool for about 20 minutes before serving.

• This recipe works well indoors when the rain comes. Just cook in two stages: slow oven followed by grill.

• Shanks are gloriously messy and chewy, and make an interesting addition to any feast.

Minted lamb burgers

Every now and then you have to try something different, but in this instance it stems from a very old, established combination of flavours. Lamb and mint seem to be made for each other.

serves 6

1 large onion, very finely chopped

3 tbsp unsalted butter

1kg roughly minced lean lamb

1 bunch of mint, finely chopped

1 garlic clove, finely chopped

2 tsp sea salt

Freshly ground black pepper

1 Soften the onion in the butter over a gentle heat – there is a lot of molten butter, but this will help make the lamb burgers hold together.

2 Add the contents of the pan to the meat in a large bowl. Add the mint and garlic.

3 Sprinkle with the salt and a few twists of freshly ground black pepper. Mix together gently, being careful not to overwork the meat. Divide into 12 flat-ish burgers and set aside in the refrigerator, covered, to mature for an hour.

4 To cook the lamb burgers, you will need a barbecue where the heat is somewhere between medium and hot. Give them 4 minutes on the first side, being sure to get a good seal that will hold the meat together. Then turn and give them another 5–7 minutes. Rest the burgers for 4 minutes before serving.

- These hamburgers work perfectly indoors; either pan-fry or grill them.
- There is an affinity between lamb burgers and wholemeal brown rolls.
- These burgers go well with the barbecue sauce on page 147.

Ginger and coriander chops

There is a restaurant in North London with such a formidable reputation for its tandoori chops that, despite their being listed as a starter, diners work their way through three portions and leave! This irritates the chef, who yearns to show off his other dishes. Naturally, his recipe for chops is a secret. But then so was this recipe – until now. Use best end of neck chops and ask your butcher to cut them two rib bones per chop.

serves 6

100g fresh root ginger	**2 small hot green chillies, deseeded**
75ml vegetable oil	**150ml thick yoghurt**
1 ripe papaya, peeled	**12 double-thick, dual-boned best end of**
1 bunch of fresh coriander,	**neck lamb chops**
finely chopped	**2 tbsp unsalted butter, melted**
100g frozen spinach, thawed	**Sea salt**

1 Make the marinade, either by using a pestle and mortar or preferably a liquidizer. Peel the ginger, chop it, and add to the liquidizer. Whizz to a paste with half the oil.
2 Add the papaya flesh to the mix and whizz some more. Add the coriander and spinach and the rest of the oil and whizz again.
3 Roughly chop the chillies and add to the liquidizer along with the yoghurt. Whizz until you have an even mixture.
4 Cut off one bone from each chop so that you end up with a single bone attached to a double-size nugget of meat. Wrap in cling film and tap with a mallet or rolling pin to flatten out the noisette of meat a little. Pare away any extra fat. Rub with the marinade and put the chops, together with any remaining marinade, into a strong plastic bag. Expel the air, seal, and leave in the refrigerator to marinate for 8 hours.
5 To cook, get the coals grey/white – you want the fire as hot as possible. Oil the metal skewers and allow two parallel skewers per three chops so they are easy to turn. Grill for about 5 minutes each side, but turn more often if they start to burn. Rest the meat away from the fire for 10 minutes and allow the excess moisture to drip off.
6 Finally, cook for another 5 minutes each side, basting with a little melted butter. Season with salt and rest for a further 10 minutes before serving.

- This recipe works well indoors when the rain comes. Just cook in two stages: medium oven followed by grill.

- This papaya marinade is a great tenderizer (but full of strident flavours). It works well with close-grained meats such as pork chops or steaks.

Butterflied leg of lamb

This is a favourite recipe that first appeared in one of my other books, *Fifty Recipes To Stake Your Life On*. Like all recipes, this one has evolved gently and will probably continue to change. It makes a good party dish, although lamb legs seem to get ever smaller, so you can only rely on feeding four people with each one. This recipe, though, is easy to scale up.

serves 4–6

5 garlic cloves, thinly sliced

Leaves from 5 large sprigs of rosemary

2 tbsp dried oregano

2 tbsp black molasses

100ml balsamic vinegar

250ml red wine

100ml good olive oil

25ml walnut oil

Sea salt and freshly ground black pepper

1 leg of lamb

1 Ask your butcher to bone the leg of lamb; you need a flat sheet of meat with the skin on one side! Or it is a simple enough job to do yourself, particularly because you don't need the finished piece of meat to be very beautiful or neat.

2 Mix together the garlic, rosemary leaves, oregano, molasses, vinegar, wine, oils, and black pepper thoroughly with a fork. Get a large, strong, plastic bag (your butcher can help you here) and add the marinade and lamb. Then comes the delightful messy bit: use your hands to rub the marinade into the lamb. Work it in well, then try and expel all the air before sealing the bag and popping it into the refrigerator to marinate for at least 3 hours. You can now stall the cooking procedure for up to 6 hours.

3 Remove the meat from the bag and save the marinade to baste with. Put it on a rack in a roasting tin and cook in a medium oven (170°C/325°F/gas mark 3) for 30–40 minutes, depending on how rare you want the meat to end up.

4 Finish the meat over glowing coals arranged around the edge of your barbecue. Burrow a hole in the centre of the coals under the meat and drop in a foil tray with a little water to act as a drip tray. Cook for 30 minutes, turning frequently – season with sea salt and baste the meat with the surplus marinade whenever you turn it. Allow to rest on a rack for 15 minutes before carving.

Devilled lamb's kidneys

'Devilling' is an old English tradition. Escoffier used to market his own ready-made bottled 'Sauce for Devilling', but in its absence we can make our own. This recipe is loosely based on that developed by Mrs. Francillon of the 'Gloucester Training College' in the 1920s.

serves 6

3 tbsp grain mustard

1 tbsp Worcestershire sauce

**1 hot green chilli, deseeded and
finely chopped**

1 tbsp olive oil

1 tbsp runny honey

1 tsp fine salt

18 lamb's kidneys

1 Take a pestle and mortar or a large bowl, and mix together the mustard, Worcestershire sauce, chilli, oil, honey, and salt.

2 Take each kidney and slash it on each side three times with a very sharp knife – you should cut about 5mm deep. Rub the kidneys with the marinade, then put them in a dish for about 30 minutes to marinate.

3 Skewer the kidneys – three per skewer.

4 You need your barbecue coals to be at the midway point between too hot and too cool. Give the skewers 3 minutes a side, turning more frequently if they start to catch, then allow to rest and cool for 5 minutes before serving. The kidneys need to be crusty on the outside and still very pink in the middle.

• This recipe works well indoors when the rain comes. Just pan-fry the marinated kidneys in butter and the devilling will turn to sauce.

• Escoffier devilled everything from eggs to pork, chicken and tongue – so can you!

Lamb steaks with olive tapenade

The dark, velvety, oily-rich taste of tapenade is the very essence of the south of France. These flavours go very well with lamb. Ask your butcher to cut you thick (2.5cm) steaks from the thick end of the leg. This is a good and substantial dish.

serves 6

3 tbsp caper berries

Juice and zest of 1 lemon

Leaves from 1 sprig of rosemary

1 small tin of anchovy fillets and
the olive oil they are packed in

12 large stoned black olives

½ garlic clove

Sea salt and freshly ground black pepper

6 lamb steaks

1 Put all the marinade ingredients (except for salt) into a blender and whizz to a fine sludge. Rub the resulting marinade into the lamb steaks, then put them and any remaining marinade into a thick plastic bag. Expel the air, seal, and transfer to the refrigerator to marinate for 4 hours (1 hour minimum).

2 To cook, you need your barbecue coals to be at the midway point between too hot and too cool. Give the steaks 4 minutes a side, allow to rest and cool for 5 minutes, then salt before serving. Lamb benefits from being pink, juicy, and chewy, so try and assess the thickness of the steaks in relation to the precise heat of the barbecue, then make a judgement as to the precise cooking time.

• This recipe works well indoors when the rain comes; just cook under the grill.

• This marinade is a full of flavour and works well with pork or chicken.

Shammi kebabs

Done well, a shammi kebab can be surprisingly light. It also has the great advantage of being twice-cooked, which leaves much less room for mistakes on the part of the cook. The only tricky part comes when you have to form the mince into kebabs and then get the kebabs to stay together on the skewer. The flat-bladed Turkish skewers are a great help with this.

serves 6

1kg finely minced lean lamb

100g cooked chickpeas (tinned work well)

8 whole cardamom pods

4 hot red chillies, left whole

1 tsp whole black peppercorns

1 tsp turmeric powder

2 tsp fine salt

½ bunch of fresh coriander, finely chopped

1 small green chilli, de-seeded and chopped

2 tbsp unsalted butter, melted

Sea salt

1 Take a large saucepan and add the lamb mince, chickpeas, cardamom pods, chillies, peppercorns, turmeric powder, and salt. Add enough water to barely cover.

2 Bring to the boil slowly, then turn down the heat and cook slowly until all the water has evaporated. Allow to cool, then remove the cardamom pods and chillies.

3 Put the contents of the pan into a food processor and whizz to a fine paste.

4 Add the coriander and green chilli to the mixture and give it one last, short whizz to mix together thoroughly.

5 Transfer the mixture to a bowl and divide into 12. Wet your hands and mould each portion onto a flat skewer in the shape of a long cylinder. Each kebab should be no more than 2cm in diameter overall and about 8cm long.

6 Brush the kebabs with melted butter, and cook them over hot coals for 2–3 minutes, turning them frequently. Finally, rest for 5 minutes, then season with a little sea salt before serving.

. . . .

- This dish will work indoors; use the grill for the second cooking.

- This dish goes well in a great kebab feast. See pages 27, 30, 31 and 67.

Mughlai lamb tikka

The skills of any restaurant tandoor chef can easily be evaluated by sampling just two dishes: the chicken tikka and the lamb tikka. On the face of it, these are straightforward preparations – little bits of meat, marinated, then cooked on skewers. But they tell a tale and can be unusually delicious. This version uses the kind of expensive ingredients, such as almonds and pistachios, that you would expect to find in a Moghul's kitchen.

serves 6

25g shelled and skinned almonds	1 tsp caraway seeds
25g shelled and skinned pistachios	1 tsp red chilli powder
50g fresh root ginger, peeled	25g cornflour
75ml vegetable oil	150ml thick yoghurt
4 garlic cloves	750g lean boneless lamb (shoulder or leg), cut into 3cm cubes
¼ small papaya	2 tbsp unsalted butter, melted
1 tsp garam masala	Sea salt

1 Make the marinade either by using a pestle and mortar or a liquidizer. Start by whizzing the almonds and pistachios to a fine dust. Add the ginger to the liquidizer and whizz to a paste using the oil. Add the garlic and papaya flesh to the mix and whizz some more. Sprinkle in the garam masala, caraway, chilli powder, and cornflour, and whizz again. Add the yoghurt and whizz until you have an even mixture.

2 Rub the lamb with this marinade and put it, with any remaining marinade, into a strong plastic bag. Expel the air, seal, and leave in the refrigerator for 6 hours.

3 Oil metal skewers lightly before use (or use bamboo skewers that have been soaked in water for at least 2 hours). Skewer the tikkas on, but do not allow the cubes of meat to touch – when they are pressed together tightly they do not cook so well.

4 To cook, get the coals of the barbecue grey/white – you want it as hot as possible to imitate a tandoor. Grill for about 3 minutes each side, but turn more frequently if the tikkas start to burn. Baste sparingly with melted butter using a pastry brush. Rest the meat away from the fire for 10 minutes and allow excess moisture to drip away.

5 Finally, cook for another 3 minutes each side, basting sparingly with melted butter, before resting for a further 5 minutes, seasoning with sea salt and serving.

· ·

This dish will work indoors; get your oven as hot as you can (200°C/400°F/gas mark 6) and prepare for a smoky kitchen.

This makes a great starter, or serve with reshmi chicken kebabs (page 27), green chicken kebabs (page 30) and methi chicken kebabs (page 31).

Mint seekh kebabs

This is a minty variant of that restaurant stand-by, the seekh kebab. As with all these sausage-like kebabs, the only really tricky part comes when you have to form the mince into kebabs and get the kebabs to stay together on the skewer. Flat-bladed Turkish skewers are a great help.

serves 6

75g fresh root ginger, peeled and chopped

3 red chillies, deseeded

3 garlic cloves, chopped

2 tbsp vegetable oil

1kg finely minced lean lamb

1 large onion, finely chopped

1 tsp dried methi (fenugreek leaves)

2 tsp fine salt

1 tsp garam masala

1 bunch of fresh mint, finely chopped

2 tbsp unsalted butter, melted

Sea salt

1 To make the paste, take either a liquidizer or pestle and mortar and whizz the ginger, chillies and garlic with the oil until you have a sludgy paste.

2 Transfer to a large bowl with the lamb mince, onion, dried methi, salt, and garam masala. Mix thoroughly, then work the mint into the mixture. Cover the bowl and leave it in the refrigerator for at least 1 hour and up to 3 hours.

3 To cook, divide the mince into 12. Wet your hands and mould each portion onto a flat skewer in the shape of a long cylinder. Each kebab should be no more than 2cm in diameter overall and about 8cm long.

4 Cook over hot coals for 4–5 minutes, turning frequently. Remove from the grill and allow to rest for 5 minutes while the excess moisture drains away. Finally, brush with melted butter and grill once more for 3–4 minutes, turning as necessary. Rest once again for 5 minutes, and season with a little sea salt before serving.

● This dish will work indoors; use the grill for the second cooking.

● This dish goes well in a great kebab feast. See pages 27, 30, 31, and 67.

Asafoetida kebabs

Asafoetida is strange stuff. In Indian shops, it is known as 'hing' and this unprepossessing powder lives up to its literal translation 'devil's pooh'. Cook it thoroughly, however, and you are left with an impressive, savoury, rather oniony, flavour. This kebab is one where the meat element is pre-cooked – a great help to the cook!

serves 6

1kg lean boneless lamb (shoulder or leg), cut into 3cm cubes

1 tsp whole black peppercorns

1 tsp turmeric powder

3 tsp mixed spice

3 bay leaves

2 tsp fine salt

75ml vegetable oil

2 tsp asafoetida powder

2 tsp cumin seeds

2 tsp coriander seeds

1 tsp ground ginger

1 tsp amchoor (sour mango powder)

150ml thick yoghurt

2 tbsp unsalted butter, melted

Sea salt

1 Put the lamb, peppercorns, turmeric, mixed spice, bay leaves, and salt into a large saucepan. Add enough water to cover by 2cm. Bring to the boil, then simmer for 15 minutes. Remove the meat with a slotted spoon and dry off on kitchen paper.

2 Combine the oil and asafoetida and add to a large frying pan. Brown the pieces of lamb in this mixture, then set aside to cool.

3 Toast the cumin and coriander seeds in a dry pan until fragrant, then grind them in a pestle and mortar with the ginger and amchoor. Stir the spices into the yoghurt.

4 Rub the lamb with this marinade and put it, with any remaining marinade, into a strong plastic bag. Expel the air, seal, and leave in the refrigerator for 2 hours.

5 Oil metal skewers lightly before use (or use bamboo skewers that have been soaked in water for at least 2 hours). Skewer the lamb, but do not allow the cubes of meat to touch – when they are pressed together tightly they do not cook so well.

6 To cook, get the coals grey/white; as hot as possible. Grill for about 3 minutes each side, but turn more often if the kebabs start to burn. Baste sparingly with melted butter. Rest the meat away from the fire for 10 minutes and allow moisture to drip away.

7 Finally, cook for another 2 minutes each side, basting sparingly with melted butter, before resting for a further 5 minutes, seasoning with sea salt and serving.

● This dish will work indoors; get your oven as hot as you can (200°C/400°F/gas mark 6) and prepare for a smoky kitchen.

● This dish goes well in a great kebab feast. See pages 27, 30, 31 and 67.

Lamb satay

Like its very close relative, the chicken satay on page 23, this is a great restaurant dish. The difference in the recipes is in recognition that lamb can prove tougher than chicken and so the greater tenderizing qualities of pineapple are called for. The peanut sauce stays the same, and needs to be carefully balanced for sweetness, saltiness and sharpness before serving.

serves 6

½ pineapple

100ml light soy sauce

7 garlic cloves

750g lean boneless lamb
   (shoulder or leg), cut into
   1.5cm cubes

300g shallots, finely chopped

2 lemon grass stalks, finely chopped

1 tbsp hot chilli sauce

100ml groundnut oil

300g jar of crunchy peanut butter

1 tbsp fine salt

Juice of 2 limes

4 tbsp runny honey

1 Liquidize the pineapple and add the pulp to the light soy sauce with 1 clove of crushed garlic. Mix together well, put into a flat dish, and jumble the cubes of lamb in this marinade. Cover and then set aside in the refrigerator for at least 6 hours (or overnight would be fine).

2 To make the satay sauce, place the shallots, remaining garlic cloves, lemon grass, and hot chilli sauce in a liquidizer and whizz to a paste.

3 Heat the oil in a heavy frying pan and fry the paste – the flavours should be liberated but the paste must not end up looking too brown.

4 Transfer the paste to a large pan and add 1 litre of water, the peanut butter, salt, lime juice, and honey. Mix well, bring to the boil and cook for about 10 minutes, longer if you find the texture too runny. Cool and set to one side. Adjust the seasoning in every dimension – sweetness, saltiness, sharpness, chilli heat.

5 Thread the lamb cubes onto small, pre-soaked bamboo skewers. Cook the skewers over a moderate grill, turning frequently. They should take 5–7 minutes. When checking if they are done, there is no substitute for cutting a piece of meat open and studying the very middle. Serve with the lukewarm satay sauce.

This dish will work indoors; just use a grill.

Satay sauce is always a winner and it will go with almost anything you care to grill.

Teriyaki lamb's liver

The inherent sweetness of the lamb's liver means that you have to create a teriyaki marinade that is slightly tangier than usual. You must also be careful not to overcook the liver unless you like it chewy.

serves 6

400g lamb's liver

75ml Japanese soy sauce

75ml ordinary sake (you can use dry sherry)

75ml mirin

½ tsp cayenne pepper

Sea salt and freshly ground black pepper

1 Cut the liver into strips 1cm by 1cm by 4cm.

2 Thread the liver onto 18 pre-soaked bamboo skewers, each piece in an 'S' shape, but do not allow the pieces to touch.

3 Make the marinade by mixing 50ml of the Japanese soy with 50ml of sake, 50ml of mirin, and the cayenne pepper. Reserve the rest to make the sauce.

4 Pour half the marinade into a flat dish and twirl the skewered liver in it until coated. Arrange the skewers in the dish and pour over the remaining marinade. Cover with clingflim and leave to marinate in the refrigerator for 30 minutes.

5 Make the sauce by draining the marinade into a saucepan and adding the extra soy, sake and mirin that you have saved. Cook fiercely until it thickens to make a sauce.

6 Cook the skewers over hot coals in small batches, turning constantly. Because the liver is cut small, they will only take 2–3 minutes. Check if they are done by splitting a piece with a knife – it should be pink inside.

7 When all the skewers have been grilled, season with sea salt and pepper, pour the sauce over them, and rest them for 2 minutes before serving.

- This dish will work indoors, but you need a hot grill.

- There is no dishonour in using a commercial bottled teriyaki sauce. Just experiment until you find one that is to your taste.

Merguez lollipops

Merguez are small, sometimes gnarly, and often quite gamy-tasting, lamb sausages that have a North African provenance, but are a firm favourite across the south of France. Enlightened butchers now make merguez nearly everywhere.

serves 6

18 small merguez
1 tbsp olive oil

1 Thread each sausage onto a fine pre-soaked bamboo skewer, brush it with some olive oil, and cook over the gentlest coals that you can manage on your barbecue. The skewers mean that you can twizzle the sausages and ensure that they cook evenly. Cook until done.

With merguez you must have harissa – the deadly hot North African condiment. You should try making your own as it is not difficult. This stuff is blisteringly hot and will keep in the refrigerator for a fortnight.

Harrisa – to make one small pot
2 garlic cloves
Sea salt
25ml good olive oil
50g dried red chillies, roughly chopped
2 tsp ground cumin
1 tsp caraway seeds
Squeeze of lemon juice
Handful of fresh mint leaves, finely chopped

1 Use a pestle and mortar or a liquidizer, but either way follow the same procedure. Blend the garlic to a paste with a little sea salt. Then blend in the oil, chillies, cumin, caraway seeds, lemon juice, and mint.

Kaburga (lamb ribs)

About the only people who can be persuaded to champion lamb breast are the chefs working at old-style Jewish delicatessens. This particular cut of lamb can be fatty but that leads to crispy, which in turn means delicious. In Turkish grill-houses, the chefs choose lamb ribs from the meaty end of the breast.

serves 6

1.5kg breast of lamb, as lean as possible

2 garlic cloves, finely chopped

2 tbsp sumac

Juice of 1 lemon

2 tbsp olive oil

1 tbsp Worcestershire sauce

Sea salt

1 Cut the lamb breast into manageable chunks, bring a large pot of water to the boil and pre-cook them, simmer until some of the fat runs off – this will take about 20 minutes. Remove the kaburga from the water and allow to drain and cool down.

2 Mix together the marinade ingredients: garlic, sumac, lemon juice, olive oil, and Worcestershire sauce. Rub this marinade into the meat before putting it and any remaining marinade into a thick plastic bag. Expel the air, seal, and transfer to the refrigerator to marinate for at least 2 hours; 4 hours would be better.

3 To finish, take the lamb hunks and crisp them up over a medium heat, basting with the remaining marinade – they should take about 6 minutes a side. Rest the cooked meat for 10 minutes, then salt them.

It's hard to enjoy lamb ribs that are cooked indoors, but it is possible. Use a combination of oven and grill.

Theodore's lamb souvlaki

Theodore Kyriakou is the Real Greek. He runs London's expanding empire of Real Greek restaurants and Souvlaki bars and there is no better cook to have standing over a barbecue in your back garden. He is one of the most single-minded people I know, and after collaborating with him on three cookery books – the most recent being *The Real Greek at Home*, published by Mitchell Beazley in 2004, from which this recipe has been taken – I can confirm that Greeks are both obsessive and extremely talented cooks. Food is at the very centre of Greek family life and they prize outdoor cooking above all else.

serves 6

1kg shoulder of lamb, trimmed

1 bunch of thyme, chopped

4 garlic cloves, crushed

Juice and zest of 2 lemons

300ml olive oil

100ml red wine

Salt and freshly ground black pepper

Greek flatbreads (or pitta breads)

250g ripe tomatoes, sliced

2 pickled cucumbers

Sweet paprika – as much as you can take

1 Cut the meat into walnut-size pieces. Place in a mixing bowl with the thyme, garlic, lemon zest, 100ml of olive oil, red wine and seasoning. Mix well, cover, and leave in the refrigerator overnight for the flavours to be absorbed.

2 Drain off the juices half an hour before grilling, but do not discard them. In a small jar with a tight-fitting lid, combine the juices of the marinade with the lemon juice and remaining olive oil. Screw the lid tightly and shake until the dressing is amalgamated.

3 Thread the meat onto long metal skewers, brushing with the dressing. Over hot coals, barbecue the souvlaki for about 6–8 minutes. Remove the skewers from the barbecue and rest the meat in a bowl for 10 minutes.

4 Brush the flatbreads with the marinade, then dip in the meat juices. Throw them on the hot barbecue and let them get some colour, but do not allow them to get crisp.

5 Arrange the meat on the flatbread, spread some room-temperature tzatziki (see below) and some ripe sliced tomatoes, a long slice of pickled cucumber, a sprinkle of sweet paprika and roll onto a piece of parchment paper to make eating less messy.

- You can cook this dish indoors; just use the grill.
- In Greece they make souvlaki with lean pork during the winter months when lamb is unavailable.

Theodore's recipe for tzatziki

Peel, deseed and dice a cucumber. Mix with 250g thick Greek yoghurt, a clove crushed garlic, 2 tbsp extra-virgin olive oil, and 1 tbsp chopped mint. Season, then refrigerate for at least a day.

Honey-glazed draught pork

Pork belly is another of those glorious cheaper cuts that has been dragged back into the spotlight by restaurant chefs who appreciate its richness and cheapness. As is always the case with pork, there is a trade-off between tenderness and crackling. With crackling comes chewing!

serves 6

2kg belly pork, complete with the rib bones

Juice of 2 oranges

Juice of 1 lemon

3 tbsp runny honey

1 large onion, finely chopped

1 tbsp dried oregano

2 tbsp olive oil

Sea salt and freshly ground black pepper

1 Cut the belly pork into strips along the rib bones – about 3cm across. Fill a large pot with water, bring to the boil, then simmer the belly slices for about 10 minutes. Allow the pork to cool and dry off.

2 Mix the fruit juices together with the honey, onion, oregano, and olive oil to make a marinade for the meat. Jumble the pork slices in the marinade and then put them, together with any remaining marinade, into a strong plastic bag. Expel the air from the bag, seal, and leave in the refrigerator to marinate for at least 4, and up to 12, hours.

3 Cook the draught pork slices over a medium fire for 10–12 minutes, turning them frequently because the honey in the marinade means that they have a tendency to catch and burn.

4 Season the pork with sea salt and pepper, then rest for at least 10 minutes before serving.

- This dish works perfectly indoors; just cook in a medium oven.
- The draught pork slices make a pleasant change of pace when added to a kebab feast.
- The apple and onion sauce on page 148 goes well with this dish.

Stuffed pork tenderloin

This dish is something of a grandstand affair. It needs some pre-cooking, but if you get the timing right the result is a delicious balance between lean meat, tasty stuffing, and crisp bits.

serves 6

1 large onion, finely chopped

1 tbsp olive oil

2 garlic cloves, finely chopped

100g pine kernels

100g no-need-to-soak dried apricots, finely chopped

Juice of 1 lemon

1 bunch of flat-leaf parsley, finely chopped

Sea salt and freshly ground black pepper

2 large pork tenderloins

2 tbsp unsalted butter, melted

1 Start by making the stuffing. Fry the onion in the oil and cook and starting to colour. Add the garlic and cook until it softens.

2 Dry-fry the pine kernels until toasted, then add to the mix. Add the apricots, lemon juice, and parsley and season well with salt and pepper. Mix well and set aside to cool.

3 Open the pork tenderloins out with a knife – imagine you are deconstructing a Swiss roll, and make a curving cut into the centre. Flatten the meat out as best you can, spread it with the stuffing and roll it up carefully. Secure the roll with some string every 2cm or so.

4 Wrap the sausage-like tenderloin in two layers of foil, with the inside face buttered to stop it sticking. Cook in a medium (170°C/325°F/gas mark 3) for 20 minutes. Take it out and rest it for 10 minutes, or refrigerate for up to 24 hours before you want to eat.

5 To finish, wait until the coals are medium-hot. Brush with melted butter, and either finish the complete roll on the barbecue (5–10 minutes, turning) and carve at the table, or cut the tenderloin into 2cm-thick slices by cutting between the strings, then brush each round with melted butter and cook for 2–3 minutes each side.

- This dish works perfectly indoors. After the initial cooking, pan-fry the rounds.
- A round of stuffed pork goes well served in a bun as if it were a burger.

- The apple and onion sauce on page 148 goes well with this dish.

Pork loin chops

When it comes to pork chops, the first problem any cook faces is buying a chop with a deep enough layer of fat to guarantee flavour. That achieved, the problem shifts to heat control – how to cook the meat through without incinerating the chop. In these situations, the way you marinate the meat is crucial, and gentle cooking is a must.

serves 6

2 garlic cloves

6 pork chops – ask your butcher to cut them thin, about 1 to 1.5cm

Juice of 1 lemon

3 tbsp mild grain mustard

1 tsp runny honey

1 Cut the garlic cloves in half and rub them thoroughly and firmly all over the meat, including the pork rinds.

2 Combine the lemon juice, mustard and honey to make a paste. Slather this paste all over the surface of the chops and set them aside for at least 1 hour, but 24 hours in the marinade is not too long.

3 To cook the chops, either start them off with 10 minutes in a low oven (130°C/250°F/gas mark ½), or if you have a gas kettle barbecue turn it to minimum and cook them with the lid closed for 5 minutes.

4 For the final cooking, finish over glowing coals for 6–8 minutes, turning as necessary. Allow to rest for 5 minutes before serving.

- This way of tackling pork chops works perfectly indoors. Cook the chops under the grill and rest before serving.

- The apple and onion sauce on page 148 goes well with these chops. Make it in advance and you can use a little by way of an alternative marinade.

Sausage patties

In Scotland and Northern Ireland, they serve a different kind of sausage which they call 'Breakfast', 'Slicing' or 'Lorne' sausage. This is much the same sausage meat as you would find in a good butcher's sausage in England (perhaps with the addition of a little beef and suet), but cooked in one piece rather than as a link. Northern cooks contend that, because this is a sausage without a skin, it is easier to cook.

serves 6

600g butcher's sausage meat (or 12 large, traditional pork sausages)
⅛ bunch of fresh parsley, finely chopped
100g crisp, fine breadcrumbs (Japanese 'panko' breadcrumbs are excellent)
1 tbsp olive oil
50g Parmesan, finely grated

1 Put the sausage meat in a bowl. If you are de-skinning sausages to get the sausage meat, just run them under the tap – when wet, the skins come away from their contents. Mix in the parsley.

2 Form the sausage meat into round patties, about 2cm thick – you should get six sizeable patties from it.

3 Spread out the breadcrumbs in a tray and press both faces of each patty into the crumbs until each patty is coated.

4 Put a baking sheet (or old frying pan) onto the grill, oil it, and sizzle the patties for 4–5 minutes each side, depending on the thickness of you patties, until a good crust forms and the fat runs. Cut one open to check whether they are done just imagine that you are cooking sausages.

5 Before serving, sprinkle the tops of the patties with Parmesan and allow the cheese to melt into the crust.

· ·

● These patties are easy to cook indoors; just fry gently in a pan.

● Make the patties much smaller and you have splendid cocktail nibbles.

A fine pork sausage

The English pork sausage is one of the unsung heroes of the barbecue world. It is the archetypal fresh sausage. This means that it is meaty and juicy, and that the fat within allows a crusty exterior to develop, while the inside remains moist and tender. All this means that the amateur outdoor cook can end up with sausages that have a raw middle and a burnt exterior. In Australia they have worked out a solution: you can buy your 'snags' (sausages) pre-cooked for the barbecue. What is surprising is that the sausages are boiled, and what is even more surprising is that this technique works a dream. For this recipe, visit your local butcher (butchers are usually more responsive than supermarkets) and ask for homemade pork sausages. Ask that they be large (about 100g each), then take pride in a traditional delicacy.

serves 6

18 large, traditional pork sausages
1 tbsp olive oil

1 Fill a large pot with water and bring to the boil. Separate the sausages and roll them between your hands. Plunge them in the boiling water and cook for about 5 minutes, until they firm up nicely. Strain off the water and leave the sausages to cool in the strainer. At this point you can keep them in the refrigerator for several hours.
2 Get the barbecue going and wait until the coals are glowing.
3 Rub the pre-cooked sausages with oily hands and grill them over medium coals, turning obsessively until they are a golden brown. Serve with onion gravy (see below).

- Make onion gravy to go with your sausages: fry plenty of thinly sliced onions in a little butter with a teaspoon of sugar until they brown. Deglaze the pan with a splash of red wine and a shake of Worcestershire sauce. Add salt and pepper to taste and thicken with either a proprietary gravy maker or cornflour.

Twice-cooked Texas ribs

BBQ ribs are such a cultural icon that Americans tend go a bit glassy-eyed just thinking about them. There are thousands of different 'original and genuine' recipes out there, and almost as many different cooking techniques. This recipe combines the strengths of many experiments and is simple to get right.

serves 6

50ml olive oil

2 garlic cloves, finely chopped

100ml maple syrup

½ bunch of coriander,   chopped

50ml white wine vinegar

1 tsp cumin seeds

1 tsp fennel seeds

1 tsp sweet paprika

1 tsp ground black pepper

3 tsp fine salt

100ml tomato ketchup

3 whole racks of meaty pork spare ribs

3 celery sticks, chopped, including the
  leafy bits

2 large onions, chopped into quarters

1 tbsp whole black peppercorns

2 tsp mixed spice

1 Start by making the barbecue sauce. Put the olive oil, garlic, maple syrup, coriander, white-wine vinegar, cumin seeds, fennel seeds, paprika, ground black pepper, and 1 tsp of salt into a liquidizer and whizz briefly until blended (or use a pestle and mortar).
2 Transfer everything to a saucepan and stir in the tomato ketchup. Bring to the boil and simmer, uncovered, until all is reduced to a thick and sticky sauce. This will take about 30 minutes. Set aside.
3 For the first cooking, put the rib racks into your largest pot – they should go in whole, if possible. Then fill with cold water, add the celery, onions, peppercorns, mixed spice, and 2 tsp of salt. Bring to the boil, then reduce to a simmer and leave to cook, uncovered, for about an hour (a little more if the ribs are very meaty). Lift out the ribs and put them in a shallow dish. Allow to cool, then cover with the barbecue sauce and leave in the refrigerator, covered, to marinate; it won't hurt to leave them for 24 hours.
4 For the final cooking, grill the ribs under a moderate heat for about 5–7 minutes a side, basting frequently with the barbecue sauce. Rest for 5 minutes, divide into individual ribs and serve.

Chinatown spare ribs

The Chinese approach to spare ribs tends to revolve around cutting the ribs up into bits approximately 2cm square, then cooking them in a wok. This recipe sticks to the genuine Chinese flavours but leaves the racks of ribs whole, American style.

serves 6

50ml groundnut oil	2 tbsp runny honey
50ml oyster sauce	1 tbsp ground ginger
50ml heavy soy sauce	3 tsp fine salt
50ml sweet chilli sauce	3 whole racks of meaty pork spare ribs
75ml Chinese rice wine	50ml hoisin sauce
(you can use dry sherry)	

1 Start by making the barbecue sauce. Put the groundnut oil, oyster sauce, soy sauce, sweet chilli sauce, rice wine, honey, ground ginger, and 1 tsp of salt into a liquidizer and whizz briefly until blended (or use a pestle and mortar).

2 Transfer everything to a saucepan, bring to the boil, and simmer, uncovered, until all is reduced to a thick and sticky sauce. This will take about 30 minutes. Set aside.

3 For the first cooking, put the rib racks into your largest pot – they should go in whole, if possible. Then fill with cold water, add the hoisin sauce and 2 tsp of salt. Bring to the boil, then reduce to a simmer and leave to cook, uncovered, for about an hour (a little more if the ribs are very meaty). Lift out the ribs and put them in a shallow dish. Allow to cool, then cover with the barbecue sauce and leave in the refrigerator to marinate – it won't hurt to leave them for 24 hours.

4 For the final cooking, you need a moderate heat and you should grill the ribs for about 5–7 minutes a side, basting frequently with the barbecue sauce. Rest for 5 minutes, divide into individual ribs and serve.

Worcestershire spare-ribs

Since 1837, Lea & Perrins Worcestershire Sauce has been delighting foodies around the world. In the distinctive bottles with the orange labels, this thin but potent flavour-enhancer melts away in any dish, leaving the vaguest whiff of spice and a savoury tang. According to the label, it contains tamarind, anchovies, and molasses, but do not think that you will be able to make your own; this is a sauce with 'secret ingredients' and it is made using closely guarded techniques. Worcestershire sauce is, however, the perfect foundation for a splendid barbecue sauce and marinade.

serves 6

2 large onions, finely chopped

2 tbsp olive oil

1 green chilli, deseeded and finely chopped

2 garlic cloves, finely chopped

150ml tomato passata

75ml Worcestershire sauce

75g soft brown sugar

50ml cider vinegar

150ml cider

1 tbsp fine salt

3 whole racks of pork spare-ribs

1 Fry the onions in the oil until they are soft. Add the chilli and cook until all is soft and beginning to colour.

2 Transfer the contents of the frying pan to a blender and add all the other ingredients: garlic, tomato passata, Worcestershire sauce, sugar, vinegar, cider, and salt. Whizz until you have a thick sauce.

3 Rub this marinade into the racks and put them and any remaining marinade into a thick plastic bag. Expel the air, seal, and transfer to the refrigerator to marinate for at least 2 hours; 4 hours would be better.

4 To get ready for cooking, first lay out a double thickness of foil and turn up the edges to make a tray. Put one rack of ribs and a third of the marinade into the centre of the foil, then bring the edges together to make a tightly sealed parcel – you can use an extra sheet of foil if your ribs are monsters. Make up three parcels.

5 If you have a kettle barbecue, you can give the ribs their first cooking with the cover closed. They need to cook gently for about 90 minutes. (An indoor oven set at

170°C/325°F/gas mark 3 would do fine). Or adjust the grill height and feed the fire to achieve the same result on an ordinary barbecue.

6 To finish, take the racks from the foil and crisp them up over a medium heat, basting with the remaining marinade – they should take about 6 minutes per side. Rest the cooked meat for 10 minutes, then cut it into individual ribs with stout kitchen scissors.

It's hard to enjoy ribs that are cooked indoors, but it is possible. Use a combination of oven and grill.

Char sui at home

Char sui is a Chinese restaurant dish, but one that you can replicate on your barbecue very successfully – providing you do not mind having your pork a slightly less strident shade of red due to leaving food colouring out of the recipe. This is a delicacy best eaten lukewarm, or even cold, so a good deal of patience is called for!

serves 6

50ml light soy sauce

50ml Chinese rice wine (dry sherry will do)

2 garlic cloves, finely chopped

1 tbsp black bean sauce

1 tbsp hoisin sauce

2 tsp five-spice powder

2 whole pork tenderloins, about 500g each

3 tbsp maltose (or runny honey)

Sea salt and freshly ground black pepper

1 Mix together the soy sauce, rice wine, garlic, black bean sauce, hoisin sauce and five-spice powder to make a marinade.

2 Split the pork tenderloins lengthways so that you have four strips of meat.

3 Rub the pork with the marinade and put it, together with any remaining marinade, into a strong plastic bag. Expel the air, seal, and leave in the refrigerator to marinate for 3–4 hours.

4 For the first cooking, make a parcel out of a double thickness of foil and put the strips and remaining marinade inside. Aim for a good seal so that the pork 'steams' within the protective cover. Put the parcel on the grill and cook over a gentle heat for 30 minutes.

5 Open the parcels and allow the meat to cool on a rack for at least 30 minutes.

6 Run a long metal skewer up the centre of each piece of meat. Prepare the baste by mixing the maltose (or honey) with 3 tbsp of boiling water, then paint it onto the tenderloin strips.

7 To finish, grill over a medium fire, basting frequently until the outside is suitably coated, for 8–10 minutes. Hang up, or place on a rack, and allow to rest for 10 minutes. Season with sea salt and pepper, then carve into thin slices (on the bias) before serving.

- This dish works perfectly indoors; just cook in a medium oven.

- Thinly sliced char sui (served cold) makes an interesting addition to a charcuterie plate.

Nearly faggots

Who said that faggots had to be round? And while we're at it, who said that faggots had to be held in such low esteem? The best faggots are a winning combination of pork mince and offal, held together with a little egg and breadcrumbs. On the barbecue, they work best if you pinch the mince mixture onto those flat Turkish skewers, then bind it in place with some caul fat. The result is a crumbly, meaty delight that would simply fall apart given any other treatment, and the caul fat takes care of the basting for you.

serves 6

150g pig's liver

100g pig's kidney

150g lean pork, e.g. shoulder

100g hard pork back fat

100g dry-cured smoked bacon

4 medium onions, finely chopped

1 garlic clove, crushed

10 sage leaves, finely chopped

1 tsp ground mace

2 medium eggs, beaten

100g fresh white breadcrumbs

Salt and freshly ground black pepper

6 pieces of caul fat

1 Start by putting the liver, kidney, pork, back fat and bacon through a mincer. (If you have no mincer, chop them finely by hand and mix together).

2 Put the meat mixture into a large pan and stir in the onions, garlic, sage and mace. Cook very gently for about 30 minutes, giving it a stir from time to time as you do not want it to brown. Allow the mix to cool and strain off all the juice.

3 Mix in the beaten eggs and add breadcrumbs until everything comes together – this stage is a bit like making pastry. Season – plenty of freshly ground black pepper – but be sparing with the salt; this will depend on the saltiness of your bacon.

4 Mould a sixth of the mix around each of the flat skewers and secure in place with a 'bandage' of caul fat.

5 To cook, wait until the coals are dying down and grill for 7–8 minutes, turning frequently to prevent the caul fat burning.

Fish

Salt-bath sardines

If you had to design a fish for the barbecue, you would probably come up with something close to a sardine. They are small enough to cook through and, as a member of the herring family, they are oily enough to do most of the basting themselves. Think back to those summer holidays when you've enjoyed sardines at a beachside restaurant. It also means you can purchase one of those wonderful 'sardine-shaped' grilling frames.

serves 6

18 large sardines

A good amount of salt for the 'bath'

25ml olive oil

Sea salt and freshly ground black pepper

Lemon juice

1 You can happily cook sardines without gutting them – the innards add a good flavour to the fish. Start by washing the sardines. Then sprinkle a 5mm layer of salt onto a flat tray, add the sardines, and nestle them down into the salt. Cover completely with another layer of salt and set aside in the refrigerator for at least 1 hour (or up to 2 hours). This will firm the fish before grilling.

2 Take the fish out of the salt and brush off most of the salt grains. Either arrange the fish on a grilling frame, or take two skewers and thread several sardines onto them like the treads of a ladder – both these approaches are designed to make turning the fish easier. Brush the fish with a little olive oil.

3 Get the coals hot and cook the fish. They should take about 10 minutes, depending on the size of the fish – 5 minutes for the first side and 3–5 minutes for the second. Keep on brushing with a little olive oil. The skin starting to blister is one sign that they are very nearly cooked. When sardines are done, the fin on the top of the body will pull out cleanly.

4 Remove from the grill frame or skewers and season with salt, pepper and lemon juice.

- You can grill sardines anywhere – indoors or out!
- In Spain, they sometimes offer 'sardinas a la teja' which translates as 'sardines cooked on a roof tile'. We may not have the large, unglazed earthenware roof tiles, but a spare unglazed floor tile (the sort known as quarry tiles) will do just fine. Put the tile over the coals until it is good and hot, which may take 30–40 minutes, depending on how thick the tile is. Cover with a layer of thin edible leaves – lettuce or spinach – arrange the sardines, and cook for about 8 minutes, turning them with a fish slice after 3–4 minutes.

Seared tuna 'burgers'

Tuna is an expensive and luxurious fish – meaty enough to be meat, tasty enough to be fish. This recipe uses the best bit of the tuna, and so proves expensive. It does, however, taste very good! Furthermore, it looks a bit like a burger, especially if served with some chips and a slice of beef tomato as garnish.

serves 6

1 tbsp black peppercorns

1 tbsp fennel seeds

2 tsp celery salt

Tuna fillet, a piece about 7cm across and 15cm long

2 tbsp unsalted butter, melted

1 Make the spice coating by whizzing up the peppercorns, fennel seeds and celery salt in a liquidizer (or use a pestle and mortar).

2 Cut the tuna into six slices about 2.5cm thick and roll them on a board to make them as round as possible – if 'hamburger' presentation is your aim.

3 Brush each piece all over with melted butter. Spread the spice mix in a shallow dish and press the tuna pieces into the spice until it has a good coating on all sides.

4 Get the grill very hot and sear the tuna – you are aiming for a crusty outside and a nearly raw middle. The tuna slices are not very thick and will cook very quickly, about 1 minute a side. If you want your fish cooked more thoroughly, give it more time. To test for 'doneness', there is no substitute for cutting a piece open and having a look. Rest for 2 minutes before serving.

· This dish works perfectly well indoors;
  just use your grill.

Tarragon salmon steaks

Over the last couple of centuries, the salmon has been all things to all men. Once it was so common that London apprentice boys had a contract stipulating that they should be fed salmon no more than three times a week, then so rare that in the 1950s it was very much a luxury food. Fast forward to the 21st century when farmed salmon is both plentiful and cheap. When buying salmon, buy the best you can afford – wild is better than organic-farmed; organic-farmed is better than intensively farmed.

serves 6

75g unsalted butter

6 x 200g salmon steaks, cut thick if possible, skinless

½ bunch of tarragon

150ml dry white wine

Sea salt and freshly ground black pepper

1 Make up a foil parcel for each salmon steak using a double thickness of foil about 25cm square. Butter the inside, centre the salmon steak and top it with a couple of sprigs of tarragon. Pull the edges up, add a knob of butter and a splash of wine before sealing it up. You are looking for an airtight seal.

2 Cook the parcels in the embers of a barbecue, or on the grill over a moderate fire. Because the salmon 'steams' within the packet, it is hard to overdo the fish. Depending on the heat of the fire, the parcels will take around 10–12 minutes to cook.

3 To serve, open the packets, place the fish on plates, and pour the juices over the top. Season with sea salt and pepper.

• You can cook this indoors in an oven; just set it at 180°C/350°F/gas mark 4.

• You can also let the parcels go cold and eat the salmon with a little mayonnaise.

Sea bass with grilled lemons

A wild sea bass weighing around 2kg, preferably eaten the same day as it is caught, is a prince among fish. Even those small farmed sea bass are pretty good to eat. But let us presume that you are, or that you are friends with, a fisherman and that you have access to the real thing, then cooking a bass on a barbecue is ridiculously simple. The grilled lemons also have charm, particularly as for some strange and inexplicable reason they end up so much juicier than even the best Italian lemons.

serves 6

1 majestic sea bass, weighing around 2kg

25ml olive oil

⅛ bunch of dill

6 lemons

Sea salt

1 Gut and clean the bass and scrape off all the scales. Rub its skin with a little olive oil and stuff the belly cavity with the dill.

2 Cut each lemon into three – two end pieces and one thick middle slice.

3 You need a hot barbecue with glowing coals. Rub the grill bars with oiled kitchen paper and put the bass on to cook. Do not be tempted to fiddle with the fish; be patient while the skin crisps and makes a good seal – this will take 8–10 minutes.

4 Arrange the lemon slices on the grill cut-sides down, then turn the fish. No fancy techniques are needed; just free the fish from the bars with a fish slice or palette knife, then roll it over gently. That way you will stand less chance of breaking the fish. Give the bass a further 7–8 minutes. The fish is done when you prod it with a finger and it is firm, but by all means cut into it to check.

5 Take the bass off the grill and salt it.

· ·

● You can cook this indoors under a domestic grill, providing you are using small sea bass – any larger fish needs a barbecue.

Mustard mackerel

The mackerel is a much misunderstood fish. Let them get just a few days too old and they become unpleasantly fishy. The culprit (and also the mackerel's greatest asset) is the very high oil content in the flesh. With a fresh fish, plenty of oil means plenty of flavour; with a stale fish the oil turns rancid. So be sure that your mackerel is as fresh as possible – straight out of the sea and before the colours have started to fade, if possible. The mustard sauce is the perfect foil for the richness of the fish.

serves 6

6 fresh mackerel

5 tbsp mild grain mustard

50g unsalted butter

3 tbsp single cream

Sea salt and freshly ground black pepper

Lemon juice

1 Gut the mackerel, if your fishmonger hasn't already done the job for you. Slash the flesh of the fish diagonally at 2cm intervals, making the cuts about 1cm deep. Rub 2 tbsp of mustard over the skin of the fish and into the slashes, then place in the refrigerator, covered, to marinate for 1 hour.

2 To make the sauce, melt the butter in a frying pan and cook the remaining mustard until the seeds crackle and it forms a paste. Add the cream, stir and season to taste. The sauce should be thick. Set to one side and keep warm.

3 Cook the fish in a fish frame. The coals should be glowing white and you should place the rack 15–20cm from the fire. Give the mackerel about 8 minutes a side. Season the fish with lemon juice, salt and ground black pepper and serve with the sauce.

• This mackerel dish works well indoors; just use the grill. The mustard sauce is also a fine accompaniment for steaks.

Grilled smoked eel

Smoked eel is implausibly rich and delicious. This recipe makes the most of those qualities by doing as little as possible; just dressing the fish and heating it through. Very sophisticated little skewers.

serves 6

12 smoked eel fillets

50ml Chinese bottled plum sauce

Juice of half a lemon

1 Using pre-soaked bamboo skewers, thread each eel fillet in a lazy 'S' shape.

2 Paint with plum sauce.

3 Grill for 1–2 minutes over a hot fire – you merely need to heat the eel through. Add a tiny splash of lemon juice to each skewer and serve.

• You can cook this indoors using a grill.

• These little skewers make very fine cocktail nibbles.

Monkfish tikka

Monkfish is a magnificent and meaty fish that responds well to this marinade. This dish will work with fillets of other firm white fish – Indian restaurants in Southall, London, make a fine fish tikka using cod.

serves 6

25g fresh root ginger, peeled

50ml groundnut oil

1 garlic clove, crushed

1 tbsp carom seeds

1 tbsp turmeric powder

1 tsp smoked paprika

Juice of 1 lemon

1.5kg monkfish tail

50ml mustard oil

1 tbsp garam masala

1 tsp fine salt

75g unsalted butter, melted

1 Make the marinade either by using a pestle and mortar or preferably a liquidizer. Chop the ginger, add it to the liquidizer, and whizz to a paste with the groundnut oil. Add the crushed garlic and whizz some more. Remove half of this paste and set aside. Whizz in half of the carom seeds, half the turmeric, half the paprika, and all the lemon juice.

2 Remove the skin or membrane from the monkfish and cut the flesh into large chunks, about twice the size of a walnut. Rub the marinade into the fish pieces and lay them in a dish. Add any remaining marinade and cover with cling film. Leave in the refrigerator to mature for 30 minutes.

3 Prepare the second (cooked) marinade. Heat the mustard oil in a frying pan until smoking. Add the ginger/garlic paste, the garam masala, salt plus the remaining carom, turmeric and paprika. Cook for about 2 minutes to bring out the flavours. Drain any liquid from the monkfish and rub in this second marinade. Put the fish back in the refrigerator, covered, for a further 2-hour marination.

4 To cook, arrange the monkfish on a metal skewer, each piece 2cm apart. Cook over medium coals for about 3–4 minutes a side, basting with any leftover marinade. Hang up the skewers (or leave on a rack) and allow them to drain for 5 minutes.

5 Finally, paint the fish with melted butter and give it a further 2–3 minutes cooking.

● This dish works perfectly well indoors; just use your grill.

● It also makes a good starter when served with a fresh chutney and hot handkerchief bread (see page 135).

Prawn cakes

Thai prawn cakes are more usually deep-fried, but this recipe works well with a two-stage cooking process. The resulting prawn cakes are sweet and salty with a chewy texture that goes very well with the 'instant' pineapple relish at the bottom of the page.

serves 6

250g raw tiger prawns

2 garlic cloves

25g fresh root ginger, peeled and
chopped

1 tsp palm sugar

1 tbsp soy sauce

2 tsp nam pla (fish sauce)

Juice of 1 lime

Small handful of coriander

Freshly ground black pepper

Groundnut oil

1 Shell and de-vein the prawns. Mince the meat very finely (you can chop with a knife but chop finely). Set to one side.

2 Using a food processor (or pestle and mortar), turn the garlic, ginger and palm sugar into a fine paste.

3 Put the prawn meat in a bowl and use a fork to work in the ginger/garlic paste, the soy sauce, fish sauce, and lime juice. Chop the coriander leaves very finely and add them with a few turns of freshly ground black pepper.

4 Divide the mixture into walnut-sized balls and flatten them off to form little cakes.

5 Heat a little oil in a frying pan and sear the prawn cakes on each side until they have 'set' – 1–2 minutes each side. Put the prawn cakes aside to cool, at which point you can start cooking, or store, covered, in the refrigerator for up to 8 hours.

6 To cook, impale three prawn cakes on a pre-soaked bamboo skewer and brush them with oil. Grill them briefly over medium coals until the outsides become crisp – approximately 2 minutes on each side.

- These prawn cakes go very well with an 'instant' pineapple relish made by finely chopping 200g of fresh, ripe pineapple, then adding 2 tbsp of sweet chilli sauce, 1 shake of fish sauce, and the juice of a lime. Mix very thoroughly or give the relish a quick burst with a hand-blender.

- If you are cooking this dish indoors, just use a frying pan and cook the prawn cakes once. You will sacrifice the crisp bits.

Prawns on the barbie

Prawns have everything it takes to be the star attraction at your next barbecue. They are glam, exotic and extravagant, plus they taste good. Try and get large, uncooked prawns – the pinky-grey ones known as tiger prawns. If they are unavailable, use the large, pink, ready-cooked 'crevettes' and only grill them for 2 minutes a side. Either way, if you are cooking near the seaside, try the seaweed variation set out below as it works well.

serves 6

3 garlic cloves

3 tsp sea salt

4 tbsp olive oil

Juice of 1 lemon

Bunch of parsley, finely chopped

Freshly ground black pepper

18 huge tiger prawns

100g unsalted butter, warmed

1 Take a pestle and mortar; pound 2 cloves of garlic and 2 tsp of salt to a paste. Use a fork and work in the oil, lemon juice, parsley (reserve 1 tbsp), and pepper.

2 De-head and tear off the legs of the prawns, but leave the body shell intact with the tail. Turn the prawn over and make a slit (through the shell) down the length of the back, then hook out the dark intestine which runs through the prawn.

3 Rub the marinade into the prawns and lay them in a dish. Pour over any remaining marinade and cover with cling film. Leave in the refrigerator, covered, for an hour.

4 Use a liquidizer (or the trusty pestle and mortar) to make a flavoured butter with the remaining garlic, salt and parsley. Divide into 18 pea-sized balls and chill to harden.

5 To cook the prawns, drain off the marinade and grill over medium coals for about 5 minutes a side, basting with the leftover marinade. As you serve them, add a piece of garlic and parsley butter to each prawn to melt over it as it comes to the table.

If at the seaside, get the coals hot, then spread a 5cm layer of washed seaweed on the rack that is over the coals. Nestle the prawns into the seaweed folds and half-grill, half-steam them, which will take about 10 minutes each side. Dress with garlic and parsley butter.

Goan prawns

Try and get hold of the largest, plumpest uncooked prawns that you can find. This is a simple recipe and the lime juice and garlic will set the 'cooking' process off before the prawns even see the fire. If you cannot buy uncooked prawns, you can make this dish with cooked pink crevettes and halve the cooking time.

serves 6

18 huge tiger prawns

1 garlic clove, crushed

2 tsp sea salt, plus extra for serving

Juice of 2 limes

Freshly ground black pepper

¼ can of coconut milk

1 tbsp cumin seeds

1 Prepare the prawns. Remove the heads and tear off the legs and undercarriage, but leave the body shell intact with the triple tail plate as a 'handle'. Turn the prawn over and make a slit (through the shell) down the length of the back, then hook out the dark intestine which runs through the prawn.

2 Take a pestle and mortar and pound the garlic and 1 tsp of salt to a paste. Use a fork to work in the lime juice and pepper.

3 Rub this marinade into the prawns and lay them in a dish. Pour over any remaining marinade and cover with cling film. Leave in the refrigerator to mature for an hour.

4 Arrange the prawns on a long metal skewer to make it easier to turn them. Stir the remaining salt into the coconut milk and brush some of this onto the prawns.

5 Grill the prawns over medium coals for about 3–4 minutes a side, basting them with the coconut milk. To test whether they are done, cut one in half and take a look. Rest for 4–5 minutes. As you serve the prawns, paint them one final time with coconut milk and sprinkle with a good pinch of cumin seeds and a little sea salt.

- This dish works perfectly well indoors; just use your grill.

Planked mussels

In the Charente region of France, diners are very keen on planked mussels – a dish that combines the charm of a pyrotechnic party trick with an end product that is very good to eat. And in the Charente it is a relatively easy dish to put together, because the woods running down to the beach provide the fuel, and the sea provides the fresh mussels. As always where mussels are concerned, freshness is all. The technology of rearing shellfish for sale has improved and it is not quite as crucial as it once was to use only live mussels – tapping each one to ensure that it snaps shut and discarding any that are dead – but I'd still recommend it. If you use frozen shellfish, keep them in cold conditions until the moment you use them. To start with, get yourself a large plank of wood at least 75cm wide by 100cm long and put it into the sea to soak for 15–30 minutes (this will prevent it burning). Take a stout nail, about 8cm, or you can use a large screw, and drive it into the very centre of your plank. It needs to be firm as it is the centre post for the swirl of mussels that you are going to build. Setting the mussels up would make a good party game, as it requires a steady hand and plenty of patience. It is also one of those irritating pastimes that looks so easy when done by someone who has done it before! Do not be downhearted; after the first few circles of mussels are in place, everything becomes easier and the shape of the mussels helps support the newcomers. The mussels are balanced upright around the central nail hinge-side uppermost (to stop the ash falling in among the meat when they open) and they must be tightly packed. You should end up with an elegant wheel that is all mussels. Planked mussels is one dish where the normal order of things is reversed and the fire goes on top of the food. The ideal fuel is pine needles. You are looking for the long, wispy pine

needles that have built up into drifts at the foot of trees and then been dried out by the sun. They are so light, so dry and so full of resin that they burn incredibly quickly and give off an immense amount of heat. Having collected enough needles, you put a small haystack of them on top of the mussels – think in terms of a heaped mound about 75cm deep. Then assemble your diners to admire the procedure and strike a match; the burning process is short-lived but spectacular. Within 3 minutes cooking is accomplished. Take a beach towel or the lid from a cardboard box, and waft away the ash to reveal the blackened mussels, which will still be extremely hot. Prise the mussels from the plank one at a time and eat. They are delicious: sea-salty, sweet and very smoky – the slightly piney notes a perfect complement.

serves 4

Lots of mussels (say 2kg)

If this recipe appeals so much that you feel you must try it in your garden but are handicapped by the lack of a beach, and also by the scarcity of pine needles, do not despair. Follow the maritime method, but use instead a large but loosely packed mound of dry hay, and take extra care to avoid the fire spreading to anything other than the mussels. This is one occasion when a bucket of water is a vital accessory.

Scampi and bacon

Scampi's reputation took a pretty heavy bashing in the 1970s, when it enjoyed a period in the limelight, and its popularity lead to widespread faking with chunks of monkfish tail breadcrumbed and passed off as scampi to save money. Strictly speaking 'scampo' – plural scampi – is an Italian word and refers to the tail meat from a large member of the prawn family also known as the langoustine or Dublin bay prawn. This recipe works with any large prawn tail, whatever you choose to call it, and would probably work with chunks of monkfish tail just as well.

serves 6

18 rashers of streaky bacon
18 large prawn tails

1 Pre-cook the rashers, which will make them easier to wrap around the prawns. Lay the bacon out in a frying pan (one layer at a time), cover with water, and bring to the boil. Set the bacon aside to drain.

2 Wrap each prawn in a slice of bacon and thread them three per skewer.

3 Cook over a moderate fire. If you are using cooked prawn tails, this will take 2–3 minutes a side; if you are using raw prawns, then give the skewers up to 4–5 minutes a side – by which time the bacon should be sizzled and delicious. Check if they are done by cutting a prawn in half.

· This dish works perfectly well indoors; just use your grill.

· These prawns make good cocktail nibbles.

Theodore's lobster

As mentioned earlier, Theodore Kyriakou is the chef behind London's Real Greek restaurant, and someone I have had the pleasure of collaborating with on a number of cookbooks. His method for barbecued lobster is simplicity itself: lobsters, a marinade, then a seriously delicious, mayonnaisey sort of gloop to spread on the lobsters as they come off the grill.

serves 4

1 green pepper, deseeded and
    finely chopped

Bunch of chives, finely chopped

50ml olive oil

2 tbsp runny honey

Juice of 2 lemons and zest of 1

4 live lobsters, approx. 500g each

125g stale white bread

Generous bunch of flat-leaf parsley,
    including the stalks, finely chopped

⅓ bunch of spring onions, finely chopped

1 egg yolk

150ml extra-virgin olive oil

Salt and freshly ground black pepper

1 Make the marinade by combining the green pepper, chives, olive oil, honey, and the juice and zest of 1 lemon in a large jug and mixing well.

2 Take a large kitchen knife and kill each lobster mercifully by stabbing it through the cross in the centre of its head. Bring the knife down to cut the crustacean in half lengthways. Remove the digestive tract and the grey sac that you will find in the head. Crack the claws with the back of the knife.

3 Put the lobster halves in a flat dish and pour the marinade over them. Cover with cling film and leave in the refrigerator for at least 30 minutes, or preferably an hour.

4 Make the parsley gloop. Soak the bread in water until soft, then squeeze the water out. Put the parsley and spring onions into a food processor and pulse. Add the bread a little at a time, pulsing as you go. Add the egg yolk and continue pulsing. Drizzle in the olive oil and remaining lemon juice, pulsing until smooth and creamy. Season.

5 Get the coals hot and place the lobsters, flesh-side down, on the rack. After about 6 minutes, turn them over and cook the other side for 6–8 minutes. The lobsters are ready when the shells turn red; the flesh should be pink and white. As the lobsters come off the barbecue, spread them with the parsley mixture and eat while still warm.

- You can cook this indoors under a domestic grill.

- This parsley post-cooking-marinade works well with almost anything, especially fish and shellfish.

Stuffed baby squid

Baby squid are fiddly little fellows, but well worth the effort of preparing. However large or small, squid have one thing in common: you must either cook them for a very long time or for a very short time. Anywhere in between and you end up with toughness personified. Persevere, as this dish is charming by the very nature of its scale. It makes a great starter or cocktail party canapé if you and your guests are seriously greedy!

serves 6

750g baby squid

100g couscous

25g raisins

1 small hot red chilli, deseeded
   and very finely chopped

2 lemon grass stalks, very
   finely chopped

¼ bunch of coriander, finely chopped

¼ bunch of spring onions, finely chopped

25g unsalted butter

Juice and zest of a lemon

Salt and freshly ground black pepper

25ml olive oil

1 Either ask your fishmonger to clean the squid, or do it yourself. You are aiming for small individual pouches, so pull the head away from the body, taking with it the intestines. Cut off the tentacles and set aside for another dish. Cut out the little beak. Pull out the hard quill and you should be left with the body. Remove the fins and pull off the purplish skin. Wash the squidlet pouches out carefully.

2 Put the couscous and raisins in a heatproof bowl. Bring 125ml of water to the boil and pour it over the couscous mixture. Stir in the chilli, lemon grass, coriander, and

onions and leave it for 5 minutes. Stir in the butter and add the lemon juice and zest. Season.

3 Stuff each squidlet pouch with the mixture. Don't pack them tight, as the stuffing expands and the pouch contracts while it cooks. Seal the mouth of each pouch with a pre-soaked wooden cocktail stick. All of this can be done well before the cooking time.

4 To cook, make sure the barbecue has plenty of glowing coals (just about the point when the fire begins to wane). Oil the little squid and give them 2–3 minutes each side. Serve straight away.

● You can cook this indoors under a domestic grill. Deep-fry the tentacles for a crunchy garnish.

Grilled squid

Grilling squid is a very satisfying and lightening-fast procedure, as squid is one of those ingredients that must either be cooked slowly for a very long time or quickly for a very short one. As with so many fish dishes, freshness is all. This is one occasion when you should make your fishmonger earn his money by doing the cleaning and preparation for you. You should carry home a 'tube' of squid body and a few clumps of tentacles.

serves 6

800g squid (about 4–5 medium squid), cleaned and prepared

75ml olive oil

3 tbsp balsamic vinegar

1 tbsp runny honey

2 small green chillies, deseeded and finely chopped

2 garlic cloves, finely chopped

Sea salt and freshly ground black pepper

1 Cut the squid body open until you have a flat sheet, score it deeply with a sharp knife in a diamond pattern, with the cuts about 1cm apart.

2 Make up the marinade by mixing the olive oil, balsamic vinegar, runny honey, chillies, and garlic in a jug.

3 Rub the squid pieces with the marinade, cover and put into the refrigerator for 30–60 minutes.

4 To cook, shake the squid pieces free of any excess marinade, then grill over a fierce heat for 2 minutes, turning at least once. Season with sea salt and pepper, then serve and eat promptly.

- You can cook this indoors under a domestic grill.

- To serve, slice a French loaf and fill with squid straight from the grill together with some rocket leaves or sprigs of watercress.

Scallops en brochette

For this recipe, you do not need giant scallops – they should be about 3–4cm in diameter. Frozen scallops will work but have a tendency towards toughness. If you do choose frozen scallops, your first job is to thaw them gently and thoroughly. The aubergines act as a sponge to keep the scallops basted.

serves 6

24 small fresh scallops

250ml olive oil

Juice of a lemon

3 small long aubergines (roughly 2cm in diameter)

Salt and freshly ground black pepper

1 Put the scallops in a bowl and add 100ml of the olive oil together with the lemon juice. Mix well and set aside, covered, to marinate in the refrigerator for 30–60 minutes.

2 Meanwhile, slice the aubergines so that you have 30 discs about 1cm thick by 4cm in diameter. Lay them out in a flat dish and pour over the remaining oil, together with a sprinkling of salt and freshly ground black pepper. Allow to marinate until you are ready to cook the scallops.

3 Use flat or square skewers to stop the scallops slipping as you turn them and assemble the brochettes, starting with an aubergine slice, then a scallop – five aubergine slices and four scallops per skewer. Pack them tightly as the oily aubergine will baste the scallops.

4 Cook over a moderate fire for about 5–6 minutes, turning frequently.

5 Season with salt and pepper before serving.

This dish works perfectly well indoors; just use your grill.

If you want to use large scallops, cut them in half and lengthen the cooking time.

Vegetables

Cheese in vine leaves

This dish is what happens when cheese on toast meets those parcels of rice in lotus leaves that you get in smart Chinese restaurants. Or, at a stretch, you could consider calling it a mini fondue. It's very easy and very delicious, as the vine leaves give a fragrant tang to the cheese within.

serves 6

18 vine leaves, preserved or fresh

A little olive oil

400g (or a number of whole) smelly cheeses – individual goat's cheeses,
a piece of Stinking Bishop, Livarot, or Camembert

1 Allow three vine leaves per parcel, and if they are the preserved ones from jars, rinse away the brine. Cut off any stalks and check that you have the underside of the leaf uppermost (that's the veiny side). Oil the leaf, put a good dollop of cheese into the centre, and fold the base of the leaf over the cheese. Fold in the sides to make a parcel. Put it, join-side down, onto a second vine leaf. Fold up carefully. Repeat with a third leaf. If your parcel looks unstable don't hesitate to use some string.
2 Grill the parcels for 4–5 minutes a side over moderate coals, until all is molten and soggy. Remove from the grill and open each parcel by making a cross-shaped cut through the leaves and peeling them back. Eat the cheese with crusty bread.

Jason's re-planted artichokes

This way of treating artichokes originated in Italy, where the following recipe was created by Jason Lowe, who later took the photographs for this book. It's a very simple procedure and makes use of that lingering retained heat as the barbecue cools down after cooking, which gives your appetite a chance to reassert itself.

serves 6

2 garlic cloves, crushed

100ml good olive oil

2 tbsp finely chopped parsley

2 tbsp finely grated Parmesan

6 globe artichoke heads, each with a good stub of stalk

1 Combine the garlic, oil, chopped parsley, and grated Parmesan using a pestle and mortar or a blender, and reduce the mixture to a sloppy paste.

2 Use your fingers to force this mixture down between the spiky petals of the artichoke hearts.

3 'Plant' the artichokes, stem down, flower up, in the embers of the barbecue, and leave for as long as you wish – at least 40 minutes.

4 To eat, tear off any burnt-out leaves and discard, then pluck and eat the inner leaves before discarding the furry choke and eating the heart.

Turkish aubergines

The Turkish grill-houses have a way of cooking aubergines that leaves them melting and delicious. This recipe tries to achieve the same end – the juices are very good indeed.

serves 6

50ml olive oil

3 garlic cloves

1 tbsp sumac

3 large aubergines, preferably the violet-coloured ones

Salt and freshly ground black pepper

1 Either use a blender or a pestle and mortar to whizz the olive oil, garlic and sumac until you have a thick liquid.

2 Slice the aubergine into rounds about 1cm thick, lay the pieces out on a tray, and paint with the garlic oil. Sprinkle with salt and pepper. Leave for 10 minutes before turning the slices and repeating the exercise on the other side.

3 Assemble the aubergines on flat skewers, pushing the slices together tightly. Cover with a double layer of foil, following the shape of the aubergine.

4 Cook over a moderate fire for 30–40 minutes. Remove and rest for 10 minutes, then either serve straight away with the juices, or remove the foil and give the aubergines a quick sizzle on the grill.

Veggie kebabs

The idea of a veggie kebab sounds a tad dated, but even if you try this combination in a tongue-in-cheek, spirit-of-retro mood, it works well. The aim is to combine a range of textures and tastes.

serves 6

75ml olive oil

25ml balsamic vinegar

1 garlic clove, crushed

Leaves from 3 large sprigs of rosemary

24 medium button mushrooms

2 aubergines

3 red onions

Sea salt and freshly ground black pepper

1 Make up the marinade by shaking the olive oil, balsamic vinegar, garlic, and rosemary together in a jar.

2 Leave the mushrooms whole. Cut the aubergines into rounds approximately 1cm thick. Peel the onions and slice into quarters vertically (so that a piece of the root holds each quarter together).

3 Assemble on skewers, alternating the veg. Pour the marinade into a flat dish and rotate the skewers until the vegetables are well-coated, for 5-10 minutes.

4 Cook over a moderate fire, turning and basting with the leftover marinade. Depending on the fire, the kebabs should take around 10–12 minutes. The skewers are cooked when the mushrooms and aubergine are softening but the onion retains a touch of crispness. Everything should have delicious charred bits. Season and serve.

Baked red peppers

Red peppers are not usually up to much in the flavour stakes – too many come into the kitchen by way of a short life in a greenhouse, where they have been force-fed and watered; sure, they are large and glossy, but they have little oomph. This development of a classic recipe helps them along.

serves 6

6 red peppers

1 tin of anchovy fillets in olive oil

6 garlic cloves

50ml olive oil

6 tbsp finely grated Parmesan

1 Slice the tops off the peppers and scoop out the seeds and connective tissue.

2 You need 12 sheets of foil (approximately 30cm by 30cm). Take two sheets per pepper, oil the top sheet, and sit the pepper in the middle. Put a couple of anchovy fillets and a splash of the fishy oil into each pepper. Slice a garlic clove and add to each pepper. Add an extra splash of olive oil and a tablespoon of grated Parmesan. Draw up the foil and twist it shut. You are aiming for sealed packages.

3 Cook at one end of the barbecue grill, where the heat is at its gentlest, for as long as possible – 45 minutes is fine; by then you will have a soft and soggy pepper. Either enjoy the peppers as they are, or carefully remove the foil and balance them over the naked coals to brown their exteriors.

Char-grilled chicory

Chicory, which is also known as 'chicon', is one of the few vegetables that delivers a gloriously bitter taste. This strong flavour goes well with the charred bar marks that you get from the grill.

serves 6

6 heads of chicory

50ml olive oil

Sea salt and freshly ground black pepper

1 Cut the chicory in half lengthways and rub with some oil.

2 Start by grilling them cut-side down, until you have pronounced dark grill marks.

3 Finish them off by turning them over and giving them another 2 minutes on the grill. Remove and drizzle a little of the remaining oil into the cut side. Sprinkle with sea salt and pepper and serve.

Sweetcorn

The blandness of commercially grown sweetcorn is much improved by the honesty of barbecuing as a cooking method. And cooking sweetcorn is a simple procedure.

serves 6

6 heads of sweetcorn

100g unsalted butter

Sea salt and freshly ground black pepper

1 Being careful not to break them, bend back the green leaves of the sweetcorn to expose the silky threads and the rows of yellow kernels. Pluck out all the silky bits. Then replace the green leaves – you can use a small length of garden wire to twist them shut at the pointed end.

2 Bury them in the embers of a fire and do your best to forget about them; 30–40 minutes should do it. Dig them up, discard the charred outer leaves, and add butter, sea salt and black pepper to the roasted kernels.

Asparagus with Parmesan

Asparagus loves the grill. The heat drives off the water and concentrates the taste while the texture remains crunchy. Parmesan loves asparagus, providing a salty/savoury counterpoint to it.

serves 6

1 large bunch of fresh asparagus

50ml olive oil

100g lump of Parmesan

Freshly ground black pepper

1 Trim away the woody stems of the asparagus and oil the spears.

2 Use a potato peeler to shave the Parmesan into long, thin curls.

3 Cook the asparagus over a hot fire to mark it, for about 10–12 minutes, turning it as necessary.

4 Put the asparagus in a dish and sprinkle with a couple of turns of pepper and the Parmesan shavings. Keep in a warm place for about 10 minutes. Serve.

Courgettes and mozzarella

Grilled courgette slices are good, and when they are turned into mozzarella sandwiches they are very good!

serves 6

6 large courgettes

200g mozzarella

25ml olive oil

Sea salt and freshly ground black pepper

1 Slice the courgettes lengthways, about 5mm thick.

2 Cut the mozzarella to the same thickness as the courgettes, and then into pieces the same width as the courgettes.

3 Make cheese sandwiches with the courgettes acting as the bread.

4 Oil and grill. Turn as necessary; they will take 4–5 minutes to cook. When they are done, season, rest them for 2 minutes, and serve.

Sweet potatoes

It sounds obvious, but sweet potatoes are sweet. This means that they make a very good accompaniment to the salty, meaty, crunchy, crispy food that comes from a barbecue.

serves 6

4 medium sweet potatoes, peeled and cut into chunks

50g unsalted butter

Sea salt and freshly ground black pepper

1 Make up two or three pouches with doubled foil and seal the sweet potatoes and butter in tightly.

2 Leave the potatoes to cook in the embers for approximately 30–60 minutes, depending on how fierce your fire is. To check if they are done, open the parcel and prod the potatoes with a knife.

3 When cooked, set them to one side – they can rest for a couple of hours before serving without coming to harm. Serve with any buttery juices and season with plenty of sea salt and pepper.

Beetroot with horseradish cream

The earthy taste of beetroot is somehow complementary to a barbecue meal.

serves 6

200ml double cream

2 tbsp hot horseradish sauce

Salt

12 whole fresh beetroot

A little olive oil

1 Beat the cream until it forms peaks, then work in the horseradish and a little salt. Put the mixture into the refrigerator while you cook the beet.

2 Keep the beetroot leaves and add them to a salad – they taste great. Oil the beets, then swaddle them in a double layer of foil. Cook them in the embers of a hot barbecue for 45–60 minutes.

3 Open the parcels, split the beetroots, and add a generous spoonful of horseradish cream. Serve.

Handkerchief bread

As most of us are not Bedouins with an iron dome set up over a charcoal fire in the desert, we must improvise to produce those delicious, thin handkerchief breads. Take a thin iron wok and turn it upside-down over your barbecue, oil the outside and let it get really hot before cooking on it. Beware: if you give a party and start to bake these breads for your guests, they can eat them even faster than you can cook them, and you may end up chained to the barbecue for the duration.

makes 8 flat breads

1 tbsp runny honey

50ml orange juice

½ tsp dried yeast

280g (approx) strong white bread flour

1 tsp fine salt

A little olive oil

1 Start with approximately 250ml of warm water. Dissolve the honey in a little of the water, add the orange juice and yeast, then wait for 5 minutes until all is frothy. Add the rest of the water.

2 Put the flour and salt in a bowl and work in the liquid. You are aiming for a springy dough that leaves the bowl clean – don't be afraid to add a little more flour or a little more warm water,

3 Knead the dough on a board for 6–7 minutes, until it is elastic.

4 Oil a bowl and put the dough into it. Cover with cling film. The dough will take between 3 and 8 hours to double in size, depending on the warmth of the place you leave the bowl in.

5 Knock back the dough and let it rest for 10 minutes.

6 To cook, arrange a wok upside-down over the barbecue and get it hot. Oil the domed surface. Cut an eighth of the dough and roll it out – it's best to make several breads at a time as the rolling must be interspersed with resting, i.e. roll to a 15cm circle and rest for 3 minutes; roll to a 20cm circle and rest for 3 minutes; roll to a 35cm circle and rest for 3 minutes – very thin!

7 Lift the dough by rolling it onto a rolling pin like a pie crust and drape it over the hot wok. Allow to cook for 20 seconds, then use spatulas to turn it. After another 30–40 seconds turn it back, and after another 30–40 seconds give it a final turn. In 30 seconds more it will be ready. Either eat hot or keep warm in a towel. These breads are quite charming even when old and chewy.

Roast garlic rolls

These small rolls have an invisible but assertive ingredient. In the same way that a jam doughnut has a hidden jammy centre, each roll contains a clove of roast garlic.

makes 10 rolls

10 garlic cloves

1 tbsp runny honey

50ml orange juice

1 tsp dried yeast

600g (approx) strong white bread flour

1 tsp fine salt

A little olive oil

A little milk

1 First, roast your garlic. Put a suitable number of whole garlic heads in a dish and roast in the oven at 180°C/350°F/gas mark 4 for 40 minutes, or until soft and melting (just how long you give them will depend upon the size of each clove). Allow to cool.

2 Start with approximately 450ml of warm water. Dissolve the honey in a little of the warm water, add the orange juice and yeast, then wait 5 minutes until all is frothy. Add the rest of the water.

3 Put the flour and salt in a bowl and work in the liquid. You are aiming for a springy dough that leaves the bowl clean – don't be afraid to add a little more flour or a little more warm water,

4 Knead the dough on a board for 6–7 minutes until it is elastic.

5 Oil a bowl and put the dough into it. Cover with cling film. The dough will take between 3 and 8 hours to double in size, depending on the warmth of the place you leave the bowl in.

6 Knock back the dough and divide into 10 pieces. Make 10 spherical rolls and hide a clove of cooked garlic (squeezed out of its papery skin) in the centre of each. Draw up the dough to enclose it completely. Let the rolls rest on a baking sheet for 10 minutes.

7 You should bake the rolls promptly in the oven at 180°C/350°F/gas mark 4, with a tin over them to shield them from the fiercest heat. (This procedure can be carried out on an iron sheet over a barbecue, with the covering tin acting as a Dutch oven, but you may need to turn the rolls over to ensure even cooking – an oven is easier!)

8 After 10 minutes, remove the tin and paint the tops with a little milk to crisp the crusts. The rolls will be cooked after a further 5–7 minutes.

Rosemary sticks

These breads lie somewhere between a regular roll and a crisp breadstick.

makes 5 sticks

1 tbsp runny honey

50ml orange juice

1 tsp dried yeast

1 tsp fine salt

600g (approx) strong white bread flour

Leaves from several sprigs of rosemary

1 Start with approximately 450ml of warm water. Dissolve the honey in a little of the warm water, add the orange juice and yeast, then wait 5 minutes until all is frothy. Add the rest of the water.

2 Put the flour and salt in a bowl and work in the liquid. You are aiming for a springy dough that leaves the bowl clean – don't be afraid to add a little bit more flour or a little more warm water.

3 Knead the dough on a board for 6–7 minutes, or until it is elastic.

4 Oil a bowl and put the dough into it. Cover with cling film. The dough will take between 3 and 8 hours to double in size, depending on the warmth of the place that you leave the bowl in.

5 Knock back the dough and divide into 5 pieces. Make 5 individual sticks about 1.5cm in diameter uncooked. Roll the bread in the rosemary leaves until they have picked up a good coating, then let them prove again on a baking sheet for 10 minutes.

6 You should bake the sticks promptly in the oven at 180°C/350°F/gas mark 4, with a tin over them to shield them from the fiercest heat. (This procedure can be carried out on an iron sheet over a barbecue, with the covering tin acting as a Dutch oven, but you may need to turn the sticks over to ensure even cooking – an oven is easier!)

7 After 10 minutes remove the tin to crisp the crusts. The sticks will be cooked after a further 5–7 minutes.

Soda bread rolls

Like so many culinary shortcuts, yeastless bread made with baking soda has become a much-prized delicacy, especially in Ireland. This recipe for soda rolls turns out hot, bready scones that are delicious, even if it does stray away from more purist recipes!

makes a dozen rolls

400g white flour	**400ml skimmed milk**
150g wholemeal flour	**1 tsp cream of tartar**
1 tsp bicarbonate of soda	**25g unsalted butter**
2 tsp fine salt	**Sea salt**
1 large egg	

1 Mix the white and wholemeal flours together with the bicarbonate and salt.

2 In a jug, mix the egg, milk and cream of tartar.

3 Combine the two mixtures in a bowl to make a soft dough, adding more skimmed milk or more white flour if the texture is not to your liking.

4 Butter a baking sheet. Cut the dough in half, then half again. Each of the four pieces will make three rolls. The shape is up to you; finger rolls will cook a little more quickly than balls. You need to experiment with shapes and sizes as you must be able to group the rolls together in such a way that a roasting tin can be placed over them upside-down to protect them while they cook.

5 You should bake the rolls promptly in the oven at 180°C/350°F/gas 4, with a tin over them to shield them from the fiercest heat. (This procedure can be carried out on an iron sheet over a barbecue, with the covering tin acting as a Dutch oven, but you may need to turn the rolls over to ensure even cooking – an oven is easier.)

6 After 10 minutes, remove the tin to crisp the crusts. The rolls will be cooked after a further 5–7 minutes. Sprinkle with sea salt and serve.

Focaccia

It would be hard to make a case for cooking focaccia on a barbecue. But equally, there is something about the crisp and oily texture of a piece of focaccia re-heated over the coals that makes it the perfect accompaniment to any barbecue. So I recommend cooking it indoors and reheating it outdoors.

serves 6

1 tsp caster sugar

Squeeze of lemon juice

2 tsp dried yeast

125ml (approx) good olive oil

500g strong white bread flour

1 tsp fine salt

1 punnet of ripe cherry tomatoes

Sea salt

1 In a jug, mix 600ml of lukewarm water with the sugar, lemon juice and dried yeast. Set aside for 5 minutes, until frothing nicely. Then add 25ml of olive oil.

2 Put the flour and fine salt into a large bowl and slowly work in the liquid. Knead until the mixture comes away from the sides of the bowl. Adjust the quantities of water and flour until you have a coherent dough. Transfer to a board or work surface.

3 Knead for 10 minutes until you have an elastic dough. Put the dough back into the bowl (which you have oiled to prevent sticking). Cover with cling film and put in a warm place to prove – about an hour, or until doubled in size.

4 Lightly oil a baking tray with a raised edge. Knock back the dough and stretch/roll to fit; it should be about 2cm deep. Oil your fingertips and make deep impressions across the dough, then push a cherry tomato into each. Brush with olive oil and leave to prove for another 10 minutes.

5 Bake in a hot oven at 200°C/400°F/gas mark 6 for 25–30 minutes, until golden-brown.

6 Remove from the oven and sprinkle with plenty of olive oil and sea salt. Leave to cool, then cut into squares and warm through on the barbecue before serving.

Easy Caesar

Ever since Caesar Cardini knocked up his eponymous salad in the 1920s, cooks have been messing with it. The anchovies, which feature in most interpretations, were absent from the original, but raw egg yolk played a part! This recipe is spectacularly easy.

100ml good mayonnaise

1 small tin of anchovies in oil

1 tbsp Worcestershire sauce

75g Parmesan, freshly grated

2 romaine lettuce hearts, or 4 whole little gem lettuces

1 First of all, make the dressing. Put the mayo, anchovies (including their oil), Worcestershire sauce and Parmesan into a jug and whizz with a hand blender.

2 If using romaine, tear each leaf into three; if using little gem, leave whole. Muddle the leaves with the dressing until well-coated in a large bowl and serve immediately.

Slacker's coleslaw

Coleslaw has featured on so many indifferent salad bars that its reputation is in need of a bit of a boost. This is a simple and easy dish and may go some way to help the rehabilitation. Try a spoonful on top of a burger.

150ml fruit yoghurt (use the sharper-tasting varieties i.e. mango or gooseberry rather than strawberry and so forth)

75ml good mayonnaise

1 garlic clove, crushed

Squeeze of lemon juice

Sea salt and freshly ground black pepper

200g white cabbage, shredded

100g red cabbage, shredded

100g carrots, shredded

1 red onion, finely sliced

1 apple, cored and shredded

25g plump sultanas

1 Make the dressing by combining the yoghurt, mayo, garlic, and lemon juice – use a fork or a whisk. Season to taste with sea salt and pepper.

2 Mix the vegetables, apple, sultanas, and the dressing thoroughly in a big bowl.

Fattoush salad

Most cuisines have a bread salad in their repertoire; this one is something of a hybrid and could just as easily have been called panzanella were it not for the distinctive notes of the zatar spice mix, which is a Middle Eastern favourite made from thyme, sumac and toasted sesame seeds. It is available at many supermarkets and specialty shops.

4 thick slices of white bread, without their crusts

50ml olive oil

1 tbsp zatar mix

1 romaine lettuce heart, finely shredded

½ bunch of mint (approx 100g), leaves only, roughly chopped

1 bunch of flat-leaf parsley (approx 200g), roughly chopped

250g ripe cherry tomatoes, halved

Juice of ½ lemon

50ml extra-virgin olive oil

Sea salt and freshly ground black pepper

1 First of all, make the croûtons. Cut the bread into 1cm cubes and jumble them up with the olive oil. When they are well-covered, spread them out on a baking tray and sprinkle with the zatar spice mix.

2 Bake in a hot oven (180°C/350°F/gas mark 4) for about 5–7 minutes. Watch them like a hawk and take them out to cool as soon as they go golden.

3 Take a large salad bowl and combine the lettuce, mint, parsley, and cherry tomatoes.

4 Mix the lemon juice and extra-virgin olive oil to form a dressing and season to taste. Toss the salad with the dressing, and at the last moment add the zatar croûtons including the tiny crispy bits (add them too early and they will go soggy, which is great, providing you like them soggy).

Red onion salad

Sometimes less really is more! This salad is a very short step from a raw onion, which means that you must be careful just what onions you use. Red ones are best – they are sweeter than their white cousins and take up the flavour of the sumac wonderfully well. Best made when the new season's red onions come into the shops.

25ml olive oil

25ml red wine vinegar

3 red onions, cut into rings

1 tbsp sumac

Sea salt and freshly ground black pepper

1 Mix the oil and vinegar – do not be put off by the fact that there is so little dressing; it is merely used to moisten the onion rings.

2 In a bowl, rub the dressing into the onion rings with one hand while adding a sprinkling of sumac with the other. (This is easier than it sounds.)

3 Add sea salt and freshly ground black pepper and allow to stand for 30 minutes.

Green salad with peachy dressing

One of Theodore Kyriakou's most delicious salads is made with peaches and green peppers and featured in our book *Real Greek Food*. This dressing captures the contrast between the sweetness of the peaches and the crunch of the green stuff.

3 ripe peaches

75ml olive oil

25ml balsamic vinegar

Sea salt and freshly ground black pepper

1 romaine lettuce heart

1 bunch of watercress

1 First of all, make the dressing. Peel the peaches (dipping them into boiling water first will make this easier), then stone them and roughly chop the flesh before putting it with the oil and balsamic into a jug. Whizz with a hand blender until amalgamated. Season to taste with salt and pepper.

2 Tear up the green stuff into manageable pieces. Muddle the leaves with the dressing until well-coated in a large bowl. Serve immediately.

Watercress and walnut salad

Watercress is just as tasty as rocket, but you must try and get traditional watercress, thick of stem and peppery of leaf. The walnuts are spread through the leaves by being made part of the dressing.

75ml good olive oil

30ml lemon juice

75g walnuts

Sea salt and freshly ground black pepper

3 bunches of traditional watercress

1 Make the dressing by combining the olive oil and lemon juice.

2 Chop the walnuts finely – use a knife and board, as power tools grind the walnuts to mush, and you wish to retain some texture. Add the chopped nuts to the dressing and season with salt and pepper.

3 Put the watercress and dressing in a large bowl and mix thoroughly.

Glass noodle salad

Glass noodles look really good, so the fact that they don't taste of much in particular shouldn't put you off. This salad offers some grand textures and exotic flavours.

150g glass noodles

3 ripe oranges

Juice of 3 limes

1 tbsp nam pla (fish sauce)

1 tbsp Tabasco sauce

3 tbsp groundnut oil

1 tbsp sesame oil

100g rocket

1 bunch of fresh coriander, roughly chopped

½ bunch of fresh mint, roughly chopped

1 Put the noodles into a bowl and pour boiling water over them. Leave for 3–4 minutes until they have softened, then refresh them under cold water and drain.

2 Peel the oranges, then divide them into segments and remove any pith.

3 Make the dressing by mixing the lime juice, fish sauce, Tabasco, groundnut oil, and sesame oil thoroughly in a jug.

4 Jumble the noodles, orange segments, rocket, coriander, and mint together in a bowl with the dressing, and serve.

Barbecue sauce

In America, they take barbecue sauce very seriously and have formulated endless recipes ,from sweet 'Kansas City'-style concoctions to screaming hot Texas chilli numbers. This one follows the simple rule of most ham glazes and salad dressings: something spicy, something sharp, something sweet, something salty. As a rule it works pretty well. This sauce also incorporates some Coca-Cola just for the hell of it!

200ml Coca-Cola

200ml tomato ketchup

2 tbsp runny honey

2 tsp hot chilli sauce

50ml brown sauce

2 garlic cloves, crushed

Juice of 1 lemon

25g unsalted butter

Sea salt and freshly ground black pepper

1 Put all the ingredients up to, and including, the butter into a large saucepan. Stir and bring to the boil. Cook while stirring until the volume has reduced by a third.

2 Adjust seasoning to taste with salt and pepper. You can either use this gloop to paint on spare-ribs, to serve with burgers, or you can cool to room temperature and transfer to a clean jar. It will keep in the refrigerator for several weeks.

Mustard sauce

A very simple and very classy sauce that goes well with any kind of pork dish.

50g unsalted butter, melted

100g coarse grain mustard

150ml double cream

Squeeze of lemon juice

Sea salt and freshly ground black pepper

1 Combine the butter and mustard in a pan and cook. The mustard seeds will crackle and spit, but they will also act like the flour in a roux, and in 1–2 minutes you will have a sludgy paste.

2 Work the cream into the pan with a wooden spoon until the sauce reaches the consistency that you like. Season to taste with a squeeze of lemon juice and some salt and pepper. Serve.

Chive butter

Chives are the gentlest members of the allium family, and this butter adds the faintest oniony note to whatever it is melted over.

250g unsalted butter
A large bunch of chives
Finely ground black pepper

1 Warm the butter until it is workable but not melted.
2 Take half the chives and chop finely, then work them into the butter together with a twist of finely ground black pepper.
3 Lay out some cling film and spread the butter out into a rectangle about 1cm thick. Lay the remaining chives across the centre of the butter and bring it together as a roll with the chives forming a central core. Use the cling film to bind the butter into a cylinder. Refrigerate overnight to harden.
4 To use the butter, cut across the roll to form roundels, each of which should have a green centre.

Apple and onion sauce

This sauce is one of my family's 'signature dishes'. It's a simple combo of sweet and savoury tastes that goes well with pork and, somewhat surprisingly, fish!

75g unsalted butter
3 large onions, finely chopped
3 large, sharp cooking apples

Sea salt and freshly ground black pepper
2 sprigs of fresh sage

1 Melt the butter in a frying pan and cook the onions for 15–20 minutes as slowly as you are able to so that they become soft, transparent, and melting without browning .
2 Peel and core the apples, and roughly chop. Add to the pan with a splash of boiling water and cover with a lid to trap the steam. Cook slowly until the apple is soft: 3–4 minutes. Mush everything together with the back of a spoon or use a hand blender.
3 Season to taste with sea salt and pepper. Then take a pair of scissors and snip fine threads of sage into the sauce. Stir in well and serve.

Fruit kebabs

These kebabs look pretty good, and the combination of hot fruit smothered in cold cream works well. Raid the fruit bowl.

Chunks of pineapple, apple, mango, banana – you choose
Bay leaves
Vanilla sugar (made by burying a vanilla pod in a jar of caster sugar)
Double cream

1 Thread chunks of fruit onto skewers and interpose a bay leaf now and then.
2 Dust with vanilla sugar – an old tea strainer is the perfect tool for this.
3 Grill over hot coals until the sugar caramelizes and the fruit heats through, 6–8 minutes. Turn frequently. Serve drenched in cold double cream.

Chilli-grilled pineapple

There is something about the chemistry of chillies and pineapples that makes them work together very well indeed.

2 ripe pineapples
50ml sweet chilli sauce
Splash of dark rum

1 Peel and core the pineapple, then cut the fruit into four lengthways.
2 Impale each pineapple segment lengthways on a flat skewer for ease of turning.
3 Mix the sweet chilli sauce with the rum, and paint all over the pieces of pineapple.
4 Grill over hot coals until the fruit is caramelized and heated through, 10–12 minutes. Turn frequently.

Roast figs

This is hardly a recipe – more of a reminder about a delicious way to enjoy a ripe fig.

8 ripe figs

A tiny amount of olive oil

1 Give each whole fig a kiss of oil by handling it while your hands are oily.

2 Grill them over a gentle fire until they burst and are marked by the fire.

Marshmallows

Another reminder!

Any number of small children

Some long skewers

A bag of marshmallows

The embers of a barbecue

1 The children toast the marshmallows – you see that they stay safe.

Choccy bananas

This pud can make you very greedy, especially if you like your bananas overripe and honey-sweet rather than solid and creamy.

serves 6

6 bananas

1 packet of chocolate buttons, or a packet of 70% chocolate

1 Leave the bananas in their skins, but cut slits into the flesh. Pop in the chocolate buttons, or slivers of dark chocolate if your tastes are more grown-up!

2 Wrap the bananas tightly in foil and cook gently over the embers of your barbecue. They will not come to harm over the dying fire and you can forget about them until your appetite returns.

· This dish works well indoors; just use a gentle oven (130°C/250°F/gas mark ½) and cook for between 45 and 60 minutes.

· To serve, unwrap, open the peel and splash with rum, or splash with cold double cream – or both!

The joy of shopping

An ingredients glossary

To be a successful cook you must first be good at shopping. Regardless of whether your aim is a formal dinner and 'haute' cuisine or an informal and much simpler meal, if you start with poor ingredients you will have to work very much harder to put good food on the table. This glossary seeks to shed light on some of the less familiar ingredients used in the preceding recipes, together with tips as to where they may be purchased, and substitutes where appropriate.

Allspice *(Pimenta dioca)* is a traditional spice, the taste of which resembles a mixture of cloves, pepper, nutmeg, and cinnamon. Not surprisingly, such an all-purpose spice is found in many cake recipes. Allspice comes from the West Indies and is usually sold as a powder, which is made from the dried, green, unripe berry.

Almond *(Prunus amygdalus)* A nut with a creamy kernel and very useful for thickening sauces. Fresh almonds have a much fuller flavour than the commercially packaged ground almonds or the slivers sold as 'nibbed almonds'.

Amchoor This terrific souring agent is also called green mango powder. It is made from unripe green mangoes, which are peeled and dried before being ground. It delivers an intense sour and fruity taste and is rich in vitamin C.

Anchovy fillets *(Engraulis encrasicolus)* Fresh anchovies are rarely found in British fishmongers, but their tinned brethren are very good indeed. Pick Cantabrian anchovies in olive oil for preference as they are larger, meatier fillets. Even with a lengthy soak, the anchovies in jars with salt are a definite second-best.

Asafoetida (Called hing in Indian shops) This is a powder with the unfortunate, but descriptive, common name of 'devil's shit'! It does smell fetid in its raw state, but when cooked leaves a gentle, garlicky taste.

Asparagus *(Asparagus officinalis)* Asparagus is a member of the lily family and is one of the few luxury vegetables with a short season – roughly speaking, May and the first two weeks of June. Outside this season cooks have to rely on greatly inferior imported asparagus, which can be flown in as far away as Peru and California.

Back fat Increasingly hard to find (due to the decline in fortunes of both traditional butchers and of suitably fat pigs), back fat is the hard, subcutaneous fat from the back of a pig.

Balsamic vinegar This dark, sweet and fruity vinegar is produced in and around Modena in Italy. It is made by painstakingly blending and ageing a wide range of different vinegars. Balsamic can prove expensive, and it's worth noting that the cheapest balsamics can be improved by a pinch of sugar.

Black bean sauce This is a Chinese sauce made from fermented black soy beans, available in jars at Chinese supermarkets. The main flavour notes that it adds are richness and saltiness.

Black molasses This is made from unrefined sugar and is also called 'blackstrap'. Traditional black treacle delivers almost the same delightful, slightly 'burnt', flavours.

Black pepper *(Piper nigrum)* Given the amazing difference in taste between the cheap bulk black peppercorns that are on offer in the supermarket and the 'premium' pepper available in specialist shops, it is amazing that cooks don't think more about just what pepper they are buying. Look out for Pondicherry pepper, Tellicherry pepper or Alleppey pepper.

Butter With butter, what you get is what you pay for. But considering how much extra flavour you get for such a small increase in price, there is no excuse to use cheap butter. Cook with unsalted butter as it less likely to burn, and you can always add salt to the dish independently.

Calvados A rich and fiery apple brandy made in Normandy and now in southwestern England. Good examples have a delightful fruity quality.

Caper berries *(Capparis spinosa)* Chefs are responsible for the modern vogue of serving the berries of the caper rather than the more traditional flower buds – both are pickled in vinegar and deliver a good tangy flavour.

Cardamom *(Elettaria cardamomum)* The best cardamoms come from the Cardamom hills in Kerala. Each heart-shaped pod contains small seeds, and the better the quality of the cardamom, the more seeds you'll find. Look for dry green pods and plenty of black seeds.

Carom seeds *(Trachyspermum ammi)* These are also known as ajowan seeds. They are related to caraway, but deliver a strong flavour that some people have described as being a bit like super-charged thyme. To look at, you would think that they were celery seeds.

Cassis This is a cordial that is much-loved in the area around Dijon in France. It delivers a powerful belt of blackcurrant flavour and is an important element in the drink named after Mayor Kir – white burgundy coloured with a dash of cassis.

Caul fat This is the edible membrane with a lacy network of fat that surrounds the intestines of animals. It makes a great, delicious, self-basting wrap and is traditionally used in Britain when making faggots. In France, it is called crépine.

Celery salt You can make this yourself by grinding up celery seeds and salt, but it hardly seems worth the bother when the commercially made products are so readily available. They tend to include a pinch of ground cumin, which improves the flavour.

Chicken In our ongoing quest for cheaper food, no meat has suffered greater indignities than chicken. With chicken (perhaps more than anything else), you only get what you pay for – cheap, mass-market chickens are very young, very heavy, and very tasteless. Buy the best chicken – free-range, slow-grown, rare breed – and you will be rewarded with a great deal more flavour and an improved texture.

Chickpeas *(Cicer arietinum)* Also known as chana in Asian food shops, the chickpea is a tricky customer. You can soak and cook them for a very long time and find that they remain hard and indigestible (often with unfortunate side effects). One good option is to used the pre-cooked chickpeas that are available in tins.

Chicory *(Cichorium intybus)* This is the witloof, also known rather confusingly as either the French or Belgian endive. It is the pointy, white, forced vegetable rather than its green, frilly, salady cousin.

Chinese rice wine This is a traditional and high-alcohol wine produced in Zhejiang Province, where it is both made in and often named after Shaosing. It is widely available in Chinese supermarkets, but you can substitute dry sherry with some success.

Chives The humble chive doesn't get the credit it deserves. It adds pretty green flecks and an agreeably gentle oniony note to flavours. Avoid the trap of 'Chinese chives', which are not the same as British chives at all,

Cinnamon sticks *(Cinnamomum verum)* Using a genuine cinnamon 'quill' – the curled inner bark does resemble a giant quill – gives a much better flavour than the ready-ground powder available in supermarkets. Cassia bark ('false cinnamon' that is sometimes touted as a possible substitute) lacks the depth of flavour you get from the real thing.

Coconut milk This is a creamy liquid made from combining the inner flesh with the juice from the interior of the coconut. The thin 'milk' from the inside of a fresh coconut is not coconut milk! Unless you live in the tropics, it is best to get your coconut milk from tins, or make it by combining creamed coconut (available in blocks from Asian stores) with a little water.

Coriander *(Coriandrum sativum)* is described by some authorities as 'the parsley of India', which is not too far-fetched, as they are related. In America, this herb is called cilantro. If you can buy a bunch with the roots still attached, do not waste them, as they have an intense flavour.

Couscous A staple throughout North Africa, couscous is made from grain – a sort of diminutive cousin to pasta. Supermarkets stock both traditional and 'easy-cook' varieties – while purists decry the latter, it works well enough.

Cream of tartar This chemical provides the source of acidity essential for soda-raised breads

– its more formal name is potassium tartrate.

Cumin (*Cuminum cyminum*) Called jeera in Indian shops. These small seeds have a pronounced flavour that some authorities have compared to caraway seeds, which they resemble slightly. Black cumin is a variation that is highly prized for its intensity of flavour.

Curd cheese This fresh cheese can prove hard to find. It's a white, very firm but light cheese with a gentle tang to it. Processed cream cheese does not make a good substitute, but strained cottage cheese will serve at a pinch.

Curry paste Though not as good as curry pastes made at home from freshly roasted and ground spices, the ready-made pastes that are sold in jars have a role to play – they are adequate to add a curry flavour and save a good deal of time and money.

Dill (*Anethum graveolens*) A member of the parsley family (it differs from fennel in that dill is an annual and fennel is perennial), this leafy green herb delivers a fresh, aniseedy flavour.

Dried apricots There are a multitude of different dried apricots to choose from, ranging from the expensive organic, wizened, untreated (lots of apricots are treated with sulphur compounds to help preserve them) hunza apricots to the plump, almost juicy, no-need-to-soak apricots. The general rule is the stronger-tasting the better.

Dried yeast Fresh yeast is not always available, and following advances in freeze-drying, dried yeast works very well, providing you are painstaking when bringing it back to life.

Fennel seeds (*Foeniculum vulgare*) Made popular by Arab traders, fennel seeds are used as a breath freshener in India. The small grey-green seeds have a charming, faintly aniseed flavour which is accentuated when they are roasted.

Fenugreek (*Trigonella foenum-graecum*) Called methi in Indian shops. You can use both the seeds and the dried or fresh leaves of this plant. Sometimes you can find fresh methi in Asian shops. Fenugreek has a very particular flavour which can dominate – something that is good news if you enjoy it!

Five-spice powder This is a ready-made spice mixture used in Chinese cookery. It is widely available in Chinese stores and increasingly in supermarkets. The exact composition varies, but generally it contains star anise, anise pepper, fennel seed, cloves, and cassia – all mixed and ground to an aromatic brown powder.

Garam masala Top Indian chefs make their own garam masala, the literal translation of which is 'hot spices', but that refers to the heating properties (in Ayurvedic terms) of the aromatics on the body. In India, the composition of garam masala varies throughout regions, but the basic mix is usually cardamom, cloves, black pepper, cumin, cinnamon, and nutmeg ground together. For most purposes, the commercial garam masala available at Asian shops or big supermarkets will do fine.

Glass noodles These are available at most Chinese supermarkets (where they are also called cellophane or transparent noodles). They tend to be made from green soya beans, starch and water – you just have to re-animate them with a short soak in hot water.

Grain mustard When it comes to deciding which grain mustard to buy, the guiding principle is that when using the mustard as a condiment, smaller grains are preferable, while for cooking larger grains work better.

Ground ginger This is the old-fashioned ginger powder that used to be found in every home baker's store-cupboard.

Groundnut oil Also known as peanut oil and very gentle in flavour.

Habañero chillies When it comes to aggressive heat, the habañero claims the crown. Dried habañeros are so potent that they can be 'swum' in a stew (tie a string to the chilli, hang it in the gravy for a few minutes and remove) and still leave behind decent chilli burn. Treat with care – chillies burn eyes and sensitive tissues. Scotch bonnets are the Caribbean equivalent.

Haldi – see turmeric on page 159.

Heavy soy sauce Soy sauce is made from fermented soy beans, plus a little yeast, wheat, salt, and sugar. Heavy soy (also known as dark or black soy) is very rich and almost sticky. It is good for marinades and braising and is available from Chinese grocers and supermarkets. See also light soy sauce below.

Hing – see asafoetida above.

Hoisin sauce This is a soy-based sauce but very sweet, with hints of garlic and a whiff of chilli. It is also known as duck sauce or red vegetable sauce. Available from Chinese grocers and supermarkets.

Horseradish sauce Creamy but with a biting pungent heat to it, traditional English horseradish sauce is a delight. When buying it ready-made in the jar from a supermarket, always read the ingredients list with care. Those brands that list turnip in the ingredients are definitely second-best.

Hot chilli sauce There are a great many hot chilli sauces on the market, ranging from Jamaican pepper sauces (generally unacceptably hot) to sauces with silly names (generally very hot) and traditional products like Tabasco (very useful because consistent heat levels mean that you know how much, or how little, to add).

Japanese soy sauce Chinese chefs are pretty dismissive about Japanese soy, which is fair enough as Japanese chefs are dismissive about Chinese soy! Japanese dark soy is called koi kuchi and is slightly less salty than Japanese light soy, making it ideal for marinades.

Jeera – see cumin on page 156.

Lamb We are all guilty of subscribing to the cult of eating lambs earlier and earlier in their brief lives. For flavour, nothing beats more elderly lamb or young mutton – just get your butcher to trim away a little more fat to avoid any possible taint of lanolin.

Lemon grass *(Cymbopogon citratus)* This staple flavouring for Thai dishes imparts a lemony flavour. It is sometimes known as citronella and is available both dried and powdered, neither of which is anywhere near as good as the fresh spikes now available from most supermarkets. Chop finely to avoid any hint of woodiness.

Light soy sauce Chinese light soy sauce is marginally saltier than its heavy sibling (see the heavy soy sauce entry, above), which makes it very useful when blending dipping sauces. A blend of both light and dark soy sauce delivers a good balanced taste.

Mace *(Myristica fragrans)* A spice that was in vogue in the 18th century, but has been overtaken in the popularity stakes by another part of the same tree: the nutmeg. The seed of the nutmeg is encased in a frilly red skirt, which is the mace. When ground, it delivers a softer, less acrid taste than the nutmeg.

Maltose A sweet malt extract that you can buy in Chinese supermarkets. It has a rounded toffee-like taste and is somehow sweet in a less obvious way than other sugars.

Methi – see fenugreek on page 156.

Mirin This is sometimes know as cooking sake, although it is not really sake at all. Mirin is made from a spirit which is combined with rice and the same bacterial culture that is used to make soy and miso. It is sweet and retains a high alcohol content that burns off during cooking to leave a sweet-savoury rich taste. Available in Japanese stores and supermarkets.

Mixed spice This is a pre-mixed spice blend that features widely in English baking – particularly cakes and biscuits. The proportions vary but the constituent parts are ground ginger, nutmeg, cinnamon, and cloves.

Muscovado sugar Unrefined, dark sugar with a rich taste. A much greater depth of flavour than refined white sugar.

Mustard oil This oil is widely used by South Indian cooks and, when raw, is very fierce indeed. To tame the flavours, simply heat the oil to smoking point, then allow to cool. Available from Asian stores and supermarkets.

Nam pla This is Thai fish sauce and is a spiritual cousin of the Malay delicacy blachan (shrimp paste) and liquamen (the fish sauce of ancient Rome). It is a magical condiment, as the fishiness seems to cook out entirely leaving just a savoury accent.

Oyster sauce An extremely savoury Chinese bottled sauce that is made from oysters and spices. You can buy it at Chinese stores and supermarkets, but it must be kept in the refrigerator when opened.

Panko breadcrumbs Available from Japanese stores, these breadcrumbs have become a firm favourite among leading chefs. They are crisper and a little bit more angular than other breadcrumbs, which enables cooks to achieve a drier, crisper coating.

Papaya *(Carica papaya)* Originally from South America, the papaya has spread across the world, partly because it is a delicious fruit to eat, and partly because it contains papain, a powerful digestive enzyme. This makes it king of all marinades.

Peanut butter Buy a good-quality crunchy peanut butter for cooking. This is one occasion when brands labelled 'organic' are often genuinely superior.

Pistachios For the very best pistachios, seek out Iranian or Middle Eastern supermarkets – they will still be expensive but not quite so expensive.

Plum sauce This is a bottled sauce for use in cooking and is available from Chinese shops and supermarkets. It is a thick sauce, almost like a jam, and is made from plums, preserved ginger, chilli, spices, vinegar, and sugar. It is useful, because it is not over-sweet.

Pork When shopping for pork, welfare issues should be uppermost in the cook's mind. Mass-produced pork is flabby, wet and pale. 'Organic pork', 'rare-breed pork' and 'free-range pork' tend to be darker, firmer, with a better fat to lean ratio. It may be more expensive, but it is well worth the extra!

Pork sausage The traditional pork sausage is one of the crowning glories of British butchery. Find a local butcher who takes real pride in his work and you will almost certainly find good, meaty sausages that are better in every way than the finest premium brands the supermarkets have to offer.

Red chilli powder This is the hot stuff and it can sometimes prove to be rather too fierce and too coarse. Buy a reputable brand and, like all spices, replace regularly before it becomes stale.

Rice-wine vinegar This vinegar is sold in Japanese stores and supermarkets. It is lower in acidity than Western vinegars and so works well in marinades and dips.

Root ginger When buying root ginger at the supermarket, choose large and fresh pieces as they are not only easier to peel, but also juicier.

Runny honey Pick new season's honey. But if you do end up with a jar of crystallized honey from the back of the store-cupboard, simply give it a minimal burst in the microwave and it will return to its runny state – do not overdo it, though, as the honey can taste caramelized.

Saffron This is the most expensive spice in the world and you get what you pay for, so if you are offered very cheap saffron, it is probably faked or at least adulterated with something cheaper, such as turmeric.

Sake This Japanese rice wine comes in as many varieties, qualities and price ranges as fine wine. Cooks should look for straightforward sake – you wouldn't cook with First Growth claret! You can substitute dry sherry, but it doesn't give the same results.

Salmon Unless you fish for salmon, or know someone who does, wild salmon will prove unreasonably expensive and very difficult to find. But wild salmon is best. Organic farmed salmon that has been farmed in the open sea (and thus has taken some exercise) is second-best. Mass-produced farmed salmon is the least successful option. The wild fish has a firmer texture and evenly spread fat; the organic salmon is less fit and more fatty; the factory farmed is the flabbiest and fattiest of all.

Scotch bonnet chillies – see habañero chillies on page 156.

Sea salt This salt comes in large and delicate crystals which somehow gives it a more intense taste, as well as delivering a delightful crunch when used as a final dressing.

Sesame oil The Chinese call this 'fragrant oil' and it is certainly a very rich and intensely nutty addition to dressings and marinades. You will find it in supermarkets and Chinese shops.

Sesame seeds These seeds are highly prized in

Japanese cookery. They are high in calcium and sometimes toasted and ground up with salt to make 'gomashio' sesame salt. The seeds come in both black and white varieties, which can prove helpful with presentation.

Smoked eel Implausibly rich and implausibly delicious, good smoked eel has enough natural fat to lubricate any secondary cooking. It is available at good delicatessens and supermarkets.

Smoked paprika In Spain, sweet paprika is known as 'pimentón' and comes in many guises: hot, mild, and smoked. The beautiful pimentón tins are works of art and you'll find them in delicatessens and Spanish stores.

Steak There have been whole books written about choosing and buying steak. Shopping principles are straightforward: slow-grown, long-matured steak is better than pink, fresh meat. The presence of marbling of fat throughout lean meat is a good thing. The steak sold by traditional butchers is almost always better quality than that pre-packed in trays for supermarkets, if only because it's cut to order.

Strong white bread flour When making bread, there is no substitute for strong white bread flour, simply because it is high in gluten and that makes for a better-textured loaf.

Sumac (*Rhus coriaria*) This spice is made from powdered dried red berries of a shrub grown in the Middle East. It has a pleasant, slightly sour, taste. Ground sumac is available from Turkish and Middle Eastern shops.

Sweet chilli sauce There is a wide range of both Chinese and Thai sweet chilli dipping sauces available at supermarkets or Chinese stores.

Sweet paprika – see smoked paprika, above.

Sweet potato (*Ipomoea batatas)* This is another plant that originated in South America, and it is sometimes mistakenly called a yam. The orange-fleshed variety, whose flesh softens when cooked, is the best buy.

Tarragon (*Artemisia dracunculus* var. *sativa)* There are two kinds of tarragon: French and Russian. The French one (var. *sativa*) is the best for cooking and imparts a gentle aniseed flavour. Best used fresh.

Tomato passata A seedless purée of tomatoes. Where once cooks relied upon a dollop of very strong, concentrated tomato paste, there is now the intense, but less acrid, Italian passata. If you come across the Greek equivalent, tomato perasti, it is often very good indeed.

Turmeric (*Curcuma longa*) Called haldi in Indian shops. Turmeric is a rock-hard rhizome with a yellow interior. Ground finely, it is a key ingredient in most commercial curry powders, and has a particular affinity with fish. It is also valued for its antiseptic properties.

V8 Juice A branded tomato juice that claims to include the juice of seven other vegetables, hence the name. The presence of the celery juice helps increase the savoury elements of the overall taste.

Vine leaves As it is very hard to find fresh vine leaves whenever you need them, it is best to rely on preserved ones. The best of these are young leaves that have been packed into jars with brine – they tend to be rather less tough than the vacuum-packed salted leaves. You'll find a range in most supermarkets.

Worcestershire sauce Messrs. Lea & Perrins Worcestershire Sauce is a one-off. For once 'the original and genuine' means just what it says, and similar bottled sauces (often called 'Worcester' sauce) are nowhere near as good.

Yoghurt When cooking or marinating with yoghurt, there are a couple of points to bear in mind: live yoghurt is better than pasteurized; and thick yoghurt is better than thin.

Zatar spice mix This is a Middle Eastern spice mix, the principle ingredients of which are wild thyme and sumac (sometimes with the addition of some sesame seeds). In Lebanon, it is sprinkled over fried eggs.

Index